GOODSON MUMBA

The EFFICIENCY BLUEPRINT

Building Systems For Sustainable Success

Copyright © 2024 by Goodson Mumba

All rights reserved. No part of this publication may be reproduced, stored or transmitted in any form or by any means, electronic, mechanical, photocopying, recording, scanning, or otherwise without written permission from the publisher. It is illegal to copy this book, post it to a website, or distribute it by any other means without permission.

First edition

ISBN: 9798334414792

This book was professionally typeset on Reedsy. Find out more at reedsy.com

Contents

Preface iv
Acknowledgement vi
Dedication vii
Disclaimer viii
1. Chapter 1: Introduction to Efficiency 1
2. Chapter 2: Assessing Current Processes 10
3. Chapter 3: Designing Effective Systems 19
4. Chapter 4: Implementing Efficient Practices 35
5. Chapter 5: Leveraging Technology for Efficiency 47
6. Chapter 6: Cultivating a Culture of Efficiency 57
7. Chapter 7: Measuring and Monitoring Progress 66
8. Chapter 8: Overcoming Common Challenges 77
9. Chapter 9: Scaling Efficiency for Growth 86
10. Chapter 10: Sustainability and Efficiency 95
11. Chapter 11: Case Studies in Efficiency 105
12. Chapter 12: Future Trends in Efficiency 114
13. Chapter 13: Continuous Improvement 125
14. Chapter 14: Building Resilience Through Efficiency 135
15. Chapter 15: The Future of Efficiency: Towards Sustainable... 146

About the Author 155

Preface

Welcome to "The Efficiency Blueprint: Building Systems For Sustainable Success."

In today's fast-paced and ever-changing world, the pursuit of efficiency has become more than just a business strategy—it's a necessity for survival and a key driver of sustainable success. Organizations across industries are constantly striving to do more with less, to streamline operations, and to maximize productivity while minimizing waste.

This book is a comprehensive guide to navigating the complexities of efficiency and building systems that not only drive performance but also promote long-term sustainability. Whether you're a seasoned executive, an aspiring entrepreneur, or a student eager to learn, the principles and strategies outlined within these pages will empower you to unlock your organization's full potential and achieve lasting success.

Through a blend of practical insights, real-world examples, and actionable advice, we'll explore every aspect of the efficiency journey—from defining objectives and mapping workflows to leveraging technology and fostering a culture of continuous improvement. Along the way, you'll discover how to overcome common challenges, adapt to emerging trends, and lead with purpose and vision.

But this book is more than just a manual for efficiency—it's a call to action. It's a reminder that each of us has the power to drive positive change within our organizations and beyond. By embracing the principles of efficiency and sustainability, we can create a future that is not only prosperous but also equitable, inclusive, and environmentally responsible.

As you embark on this journey, I encourage you to approach each chapter with an open mind and a willingness to learn. Be prepared to challenge your assumptions, rethink your approach, and embrace new ideas. And remember, the path to sustainable success is not always easy, but with dedication, perseverance, and a willingness to innovate, anything is possible.

Thank you for joining me on this journey towards building a more efficient and sustainable future. Together, let's create a blueprint for success that stands the test of time.

Warm regards,

Goodson Mumba

Acknowledgement

I would like to eternally and gratefully acknowledge the Almighty God for the infinite intelligence from His universal mind where we draw from all that we come to know and are yet to know. May I also acknowledge and thank everyone that has played a part in my journey of life in terms of spiritual, moral, emotional and material support.

Dedication

I extend my sincerest gratitude to my beloved wife, Edith Mumba, and our children, Angelina, Lubuto, Letticia, Lulumbi, and Butusho, for their unwavering support and understanding throughout the conception, writing, and eventual publication of this book, despite the sacrifices and challenges they endured.

Disclaimer

This book is a work of fiction. Names, characters, businesses, places, events, and incidents are either the products of the author's imagination or used in a fictitious manner. Any resemblance to actual persons, living or dead, or actual events is purely coincidental.

1

Chapter 1: Introduction to Efficiency

Understanding the Importance of Efficiency

With Sarah's guidance, Alex delves deeper into the concept of efficiency, eager to unravel its significance within the context of his role as the Director of Human Resources.

As they sit down to discuss the first subpoint of their efficiency journey, Sarah wastes no time in getting to the heart of the matter. "Efficiency isn't just about doing things faster or cheaper," she begins, her voice tinged with conviction. "It's about maximizing resources and achieving the greatest possible outcome with the least amount of effort."

As Alex absorbs her words, he can't help but think back to the countless hours wasted on mundane tasks and bureaucratic red tape. The realization dawns on him that inefficiency not only hampers productivity but also drains valuable time and energy that could be better spent on strategic initiatives.

Sarah continues to paint a vivid picture of the transformative power of efficiency, citing examples from her own career where small changes led to significant improvements in performance and profitability. "Efficiency isn't just a buzzword," she asserts. "It's the cornerstone of sustainable success."

Inspired by her passion and clarity of vision, Alex feels a newfound sense of purpose ignite within him. Gone are the doubts and uncertainties that plagued him earlier. With Sarah's mentorship, he is determined to lead his department on a journey towards efficiency, one that will not only benefit the company but also empower his team to reach their full potential.

As they conclude their discussion, Alex feels a sense of gratitude towards Sarah for her unwavering support and guidance. With each passing moment, he becomes more convinced that she holds the key to unlocking the secrets of success that have eluded him for so long.

Armed with a newfound understanding of the importance of efficiency, Alex is ready to tackle the challenges that lie ahead. The journey may be daunting, but with Sarah by his side, he knows that anything is possible. Together, they will build a blueprint for success that will stand the test of time.

Exploring the Benefits of Building Efficient Systems

As Sarah and Alex delve into the second subpoint of their discussion, the air crackles with anticipation. Sarah leans forward, her eyes alight with enthusiasm as she begins to unravel the myriad benefits of building efficient systems.

"Efficiency isn't just about making things easier for ourselves," Sarah explains, her voice brimming with conviction. "It's about creating a ripple effect that touches every aspect of the

CHAPTER 1: INTRODUCTION TO EFFICIENCY

organization, from productivity and profitability to employee morale and customer satisfaction."

As Alex listens intently, he can't help but feel a surge of excitement coursing through his veins. The idea that their efforts towards efficiency could have such far-reaching consequences fills him with a sense of purpose and determination.

Sarah goes on to illustrate her point with vivid examples from her own experiences, recounting how streamlining processes and eliminating waste led to exponential growth and success for the companies she worked with. "Efficiency isn't just a means to an end," she asserts. "It's a catalyst for innovation and growth."

As the conversation unfolds, Alex finds himself nodding in agreement, his mind racing with possibilities. The prospect of creating a more efficient HR department, one that not only drives results but also fosters a culture of excellence, fills him with a renewed sense of purpose.

With Sarah's guidance, Alex begins to see the benefits of building efficient systems in a whole new light. No longer just a theoretical concept, efficiency becomes a tangible goal, one that holds the promise of transforming the very fabric of the organization.

As they wrap up their discussion, Alex feels a sense of gratitude towards Sarah for opening his eyes to the potential that lies within their grasp. With her wisdom and guidance, he knows that they can achieve anything they set their minds to.

Armed with a newfound understanding of the benefits of efficiency, Alex is more determined than ever to lead his department on a journey towards success. The path may be challenging, but with Sarah by his side, he knows that they can overcome any obstacle that stands in their way.

Common Misconceptions About Efficiency

As Sarah and Alex dive into the third subpoint of their discussion, a sense of intrigue fills the room. Sarah leans forward, her expression thoughtful as she begins to address the common misconceptions surrounding efficiency.

"Efficiency is often misunderstood," Sarah begins, her voice steady yet authoritative. "Many people equate it with cutting corners or sacrificing quality for the sake of speed. But in reality, true efficiency is about finding the optimal balance between effectiveness and resource utilization."

Alex nods in agreement, recognizing the validity of Sarah's words. He recalls moments in his career where shortcuts and quick fixes led to long-term complications and setbacks, reinforcing the importance of approaching efficiency with a strategic mindset.

Sarah goes on to dispel other common myths about efficiency, drawing from her own experiences to illustrate her points. "Efficiency is not a one-size-fits-all solution," she explains. "It requires careful analysis and thoughtful consideration of the unique needs and challenges facing each organization."

As Alex listens intently, he feels a sense of relief wash over him. For too long, he had been burdened by the misconception that efficiency was synonymous with rigidity and inflexibility. But now, thanks to Sarah's guidance, he realizes that true efficiency is about adaptability and innovation.

With each passing moment, Alex's understanding of efficiency deepens, fueled by Sarah's wisdom and insight. Together, they explore the intricacies of building efficient systems, dissecting the complexities and nuances that often go overlooked.

As they conclude their discussion, Alex feels a sense of clarity and purpose settle over him. With Sarah's guidance, he is more equipped than ever to lead his department on a journey towards efficiency, armed with the knowledge and understanding to overcome any misconceptions that may stand in their way.

With renewed determination, Alex looks to the future with optimism, knowing that the path to sustainable success begins with dispelling the myths and misconceptions surrounding efficiency. And with Sarah by his side, he is ready to face whatever challenges lie ahead, confident in their ability to overcome them together.

The Impact of Inefficiency on Productivity and Success

Eager to delve into the fourth subpoint of their discussion, Sarah suggests a change of scenery for their meeting. She proposes meeting at a cozy café downtown, where they can enjoy a change of pace and fresh perspectives. Alex readily agrees, sensing the potential for inspiration in the bustling atmosphere of the city streets.

As they settle into a corner booth at the café, Sarah gestures to the two employees she has invited to join them: Grace from the finance department and Mark from operations. Alex welcomes them warmly, recognizing the value of diverse perspectives in their discussion on the impact of inefficiency.

Sarah wastes no time in getting down to business, her voice carrying a sense of urgency as she addresses the group. "Inefficiency not only hampers productivity but also undermines the long-term success of an organization," she begins, her words echoing off the café walls.

Grace and Mark nod in agreement, sharing their own experiences of how inefficiencies in their respective departments have led to missed deadlines, cost overruns, and frustrated employees. Alex listens intently, struck by the gravity of their words and the real-world implications of inefficiency.

As they delve deeper into the topic, the group begins to brainstorm potential solutions, drawing from their collective expertise and experiences. Ideas flow freely as they discuss streamlining processes, leveraging technology, and fostering a culture of continuous improvement.

Inspired by their energy and enthusiasm, Alex feels a renewed sense of purpose stirring within him. With each passing moment, he becomes more convinced of the importance of addressing inefficiency head-on, not just for the sake of the HR department, but for the entire organization.

As the meeting draws to a close, Alex feels a sense of gratitude towards Sarah, Grace, and Mark for their invaluable contributions to the discussion. With their insights and perspectives, he knows that they are better equipped than ever to tackle the challenges of inefficiency and pave the way for a future of sustainable success.

As they bid farewell and make their way back to the office, Alex can't help but feel a sense of optimism for the journey ahead. With Sarah, Grace, and Mark by his side, he knows that they can overcome any obstacle and build a more efficient and successful organization together.

Setting the Stage for Building an Efficient Blueprint

As the team reconvenes after their inspiring meeting at the café, Sarah suggests a change of scenery once again, this time opting for a tranquil park nearby. Surrounded by the beauty of nature, they find a quiet spot under the shade of a sprawling tree, where they can focus their thoughts on the task at hand.

With the sun dappling through the leaves above them, Sarah begins to outline the importance of setting the stage for building an efficient blueprint. "Before we can dive into the nitty-gritty of designing efficient systems, we need to establish a solid foundation," she explains, her voice carrying a sense of purpose.

Alex nods in agreement, recognizing the wisdom in Sarah's words. He knows that without a clear vision and strategic direction, their efforts towards efficiency could easily veer off course.

Together, they brainstorm ideas for defining objectives and goals for their efficiency initiative, drawing from their discussions earlier in the day. Grace suggests conducting a thorough assessment of their current processes to identify areas of improvement, while Mark emphasizes the importance of engaging stakeholders and gathering input from across the organization.

As they delve deeper into their discussion, a sense of clarity begins to emerge. They outline a roadmap for their efficiency journey, setting clear milestones and timelines to keep them on track. They discuss the importance of accountability and transparency, ensuring that everyone in the organization is aligned with their goals and objectives.

With each passing moment, the team becomes more energized and focused, united in their commitment to building a more efficient and successful organization. As they conclude their meeting and make their way back to the office, Alex feels a renewed sense of optimism for the journey ahead.

Armed with a clear vision and strategic plan, he knows that

they are well-equipped to tackle the challenges of building an efficient blueprint for success. With Sarah, Grace, and Mark by his side, he feels confident that they can overcome any obstacle and achieve their goals together.

Overview of the Chapters to Follow

As the sun begins to dip below the horizon, casting a warm glow over the tranquil park, Sarah gathers the team for one final discussion on the overview of the chapters to follow. Sitting in a circle on a patch of soft grass, they prepare to chart the course for their efficiency journey.

"Before we embark on this journey, it's important to have a roadmap," Sarah begins, her voice calm yet resolute. "Each chapter will serve as a stepping stone towards our ultimate goal of building an efficient blueprint for success."

Alex listens intently, eager to hear Sarah's plan for the chapters ahead. He knows that a clear roadmap will be essential for keeping them on track and ensuring their success.

Sarah outlines the key themes and objectives of each chapter, drawing from their discussions throughout the day. From assessing current processes and designing effective systems to implementing efficient practices and leveraging technology, each chapter will build upon the last, guiding them towards their ultimate goal.

As Sarah speaks, Alex feels a sense of excitement building within him. He can see the potential for transformation in each chapter, the promise of new insights and strategies to propel them forward on their journey.

Grace and Mark chime in with their own thoughts and ideas, adding depth and perspective to the discussion. Together, they brainstorm ways to apply the principles outlined in each chapter to their own departments, eager to see the impact of their efforts firsthand.

As they wrap up their meeting and bid farewell to the park, Alex feels a renewed sense of purpose and determination. With Sarah's guidance and the support of his team, he knows that they are well-equipped to tackle the challenges ahead and build a more efficient and successful organization.

As they make their way back to the office, Alex can't help but feel a sense of anticipation for the chapters to come. With each step forward, they will be one step closer to achieving their goal of building an efficiency blueprint for sustainable success. And with Sarah by their side, he knows that anything is possible.

2

Chapter 2: Assessing Current Processes

Identifying Bottlenecks and Inefficiencies

As the sun sets on another day of intense scrutiny, Alex and Sarah shift their focus to the critical task of identifying bottlenecks and inefficiencies within the HR department. Armed with the insights gleaned from their evaluation of existing systems and processes, they set out to uncover the hidden obstacles standing in the way of efficiency.

With a whiteboard as their canvas and markers in hand, they map out the flow of work through the department, tracing each step from start to finish. As they delve deeper, they begin to identify points of congestion and friction, where tasks pile up and progress grinds to a halt.

With each bottleneck they uncover, Alex feels a sense of frustration mounting within him. How could they have overlooked these glaring inefficiencies for so long? The realization weighs heavily on his shoulders, threatening to dampen his spirits.

But Sarah remains steadfast, her unwavering determination a source of strength in the face of adversity. With her guidance, Alex finds the courage to confront the challenges head-on, refusing to be deterred by the obstacles in their path.

Together, they brainstorm potential solutions, drawing from their collective expertise and experiences. They discuss strategies for streamlining workflows, reallocating resources, and eliminating unnecessary steps that contribute to inefficiency.

As they work late into the night, the glow of the whiteboard illuminating their faces, Alex feels a sense of purpose and clarity wash over him. Despite the challenges they face, he knows that they are making progress. With each bottleneck they identify and overcome, they are one step closer to building a more efficient and successful department.

As they wrap up their discussion and prepare to call it a night, Alex feels a renewed sense of determination coursing through his veins. With Sarah by his side, he knows that they can overcome any obstacle that stands in their way. Together, they will build an efficient blueprint for success, one bottleneck at a time.

Analyzing Resource Allocation and Utilization

With the dawn of a new day, Alex and Sarah turn their attention to the critical task of analyzing resource allocation and utilization within the HR department. Armed with spreadsheets and data reports, they set out to uncover inefficiencies in how resources are allocated and utilized.

As they pour over the numbers, Alex feels a knot form in his stomach. The data reveals a stark reality: resources are being squandered, with time, money, and manpower being allocated ineffectively.

But Sarah remains unfazed, her analytical mind cutting through the complexity with ease. With her guidance, Alex begins to see the patterns emerge, identifying areas where resources could be reallocated to maximize efficiency.

Together, they brainstorm ideas for optimizing resource allocation, from redistributing workloads to reallocating budgetary funds. They discuss strategies for prioritizing tasks and projects based on their impact and importance, ensuring that resources are directed towards activities that drive the greatest value for the department and the organization as a whole.

As they dive deeper into their analysis, Alex feels a sense of empowerment wash over him. For the first time, he can see a path forward, a roadmap for how they can leverage their resources more effectively to achieve their goals.

But as they uncover inefficiencies in resource allocation, they also encounter resistance from some members of the team who are reluctant to change. Faced with skepticism and pushback, Alex begins to question whether their efforts will ever bear fruit.

Yet Sarah remains steadfast, her unwavering resolve a beacon of hope in the face of adversity. With her support, Alex finds the courage to confront the challenges head-on, rallying the team around their shared vision of building a more efficient and successful department.

As the day draws to a close, Alex reflects on the progress they've made so far. Despite the obstacles they've faced, he knows that they are on the right track. With each step forward, they are one step closer to realizing their goal of building an efficient blueprint for success. And with Sarah by his side, he knows that together, they can overcome any obstacle that stands in their way.

Gathering Feedback from Stakeholders

As the sun sets on another busy day at the office, Alex and Sarah gather their thoughts and prepare to tackle the crucial task of gathering feedback from stakeholders within the organization. Armed with notepads and pens, they set out to engage with employees at all levels, from frontline staff to senior executives, to gain valuable insights into the department's operations.

Their first stop is the bustling open-plan workspace, where they approach employees with friendly smiles and open ears. They listen intently as staff members share their thoughts and experiences, offering candid feedback on the challenges they face and the areas where they see potential for improvement.

As they move from desk to desk, Alex and Sarah are struck by the diversity of perspectives and ideas they encounter. From administrative assistants to department heads, each person has a unique vantage point that offers valuable insights into the inner workings of the organization.

But gathering feedback is not without its challenges. Some employees are hesitant to speak up, fearing reprisal or dismissal of their concerns. Others are skeptical of Alex and Sarah's intentions, doubting whether their feedback will truly be taken into account.

Yet Sarah remains undeterred, her warmth and empathy putting employees at ease and encouraging them to share their thoughts openly and honestly. With her guidance, Alex learns to navigate the delicate art of gathering feedback, fostering trust and transparency with each interaction.

As they wrap up their rounds of feedback gathering, Alex and Sarah are filled with a sense of gratitude for the insights they've gained. Armed with a deeper understanding of the challenges and opportunities facing the department, they feel more confident than ever in their ability to chart a course towards greater efficiency and success.

As they make their way back to Alex's office to debrief, he can't help but feel a sense of optimism for the journey ahead. With Sarah by his side and the support of their colleagues, he knows that they are well-equipped to overcome any obstacle that stands in their way. Together, they will build an efficient blueprint for success, one stakeholder at a time.

Benchmarking Against Industry Standards

As the morning light filters through the blinds, Alex and Sarah sit down to tackle the next subpoint in their quest for efficiency: benchmarking against industry standards. With laptops open and coffee cups in hand, they set out to compare the HR department's performance metrics to those of similar organizations in the industry.

As they comb through industry reports and analyze data sets, Alex feels a sense of urgency building within him. How does their department stack up against the competition? Are they ahead of the curve or falling behind?

But Sarah remains calm and focused, her steady presence a reassuring anchor in the storm. With her guidance, Alex learns to navigate the complex world of industry benchmarks, identifying key performance indicators and metrics that will serve as benchmarks for their own department's performance.

Together, they uncover areas where the HR department excels, as well as areas where there is room for improvement. They compare their performance metrics to industry averages, gaining valuable insights into where they stand relative to their peers.

As they delve deeper into their analysis, Alex feels a sense of clarity begin to emerge. By benchmarking against industry standards, they are able to identify areas of strength and weakness, allowing them to focus their efforts on areas where they have the greatest opportunity for improvement.

But as they dig deeper into their analysis, they also encounter challenges. Some industry benchmarks seem out of reach, leaving Alex feeling disheartened and unsure of how to proceed.

Yet Sarah remains undeterred, her unwavering optimism a source of inspiration in the face of adversity. With her guidance, Alex finds the strength to push forward, determined to rise to the challenge and exceed even the loftiest of industry standards.

As they wrap up their analysis and prepare to implement their findings, Alex feels a renewed sense of purpose wash over him. With Sarah by his side and the support of their colleagues, he knows that they are well-equipped to take on whatever challenges lie ahead. Together, they will build an efficient blueprint for success, one industry benchmark at a time.

Documenting Findings and Areas for Improvement

The late afternoon sun filters through the tall windows of the company's library, casting a warm glow over the oak tables and leather-bound books. This tranquil setting, chosen by Sarah for its inspiring ambiance, is where the team gathers to tackle the final subpoint of Chapter 2: documenting their findings and areas for improvement.

Alex, Sarah, Marcus, Grace, and two other key team members, Daniel, a senior analyst, and Priya, a quality control expert, take their seats. The air is filled with a sense of accomplishment as they reflect on the progress they've made in analyzing their current systems and identifying inefficiencies.

"We've gathered a lot of data and insights," Alex begins, looking around the table. "Now it's time to compile everything into a comprehensive document. This will serve as our blueprint for driving further improvements."

Sarah, ever the organized project manager, opens her laptop and projects an outline onto the screen. "We need to create a structured document that captures our findings clearly and concisely. It should be easy to understand and actionable."

Daniel, known for his analytical skills, adds, "We should start with an executive summary that highlights the key takeaways. This will give a quick overview for anyone who needs it without diving into the details."

Priya, who has been meticulously assessing quality standards, suggests, "Each section should address a specific area we've analyzed, such as production processes, supply chain management, and customer service. For each area, we should document the current state, identified inefficiencies, and our recommendations for improvement."

Grace nods in agreement. "We also need to include metrics and KPIs that will help us track our progress. This will ensure we're moving in the right direction and making the necessary adjustments along the way."

As they dive into the task, the room becomes a hive of activity. Daniel and Priya take the lead in drafting detailed sections on their respective areas of expertise, while Marcus and Grace focus on visualizing data and creating infographics to make the document more engaging.

Sarah, with her keen eye for detail, ensures the document is well-organized and coherent. She also sets up a shared drive where everyone can collaborate and make real-time updates.

Throughout the afternoon, the team works diligently, sharing insights and refining their findings. The atmosphere is one of collaboration and mutual respect, as each member brings their unique skills to the table.

By evening, they have a comprehensive draft ready. The document is a testament to their hard work and dedication, filled with detailed analyses, clear recommendations, and actionable steps.

Alex reviews the final draft, his face reflecting a sense of pride. "This is excellent work, everyone. We've documented our findings thoroughly and identified clear areas for improvement. This will be our guide as we move forward."

Sarah stands, addressing the team. "Let's make sure we regularly update this document as we implement changes and gather new insights. It should be a living document that evolves with us."

The team agrees, understanding the importance of continuous documentation and reflection. They know that by keeping a detailed record of their findings and progress, they can ensure sustained improvement and avoid repeating past mistakes.

As they pack up for the day, the sense of accomplishment is palpable. They leave the library with a renewed sense of purpose, ready to turn their documented findings into tangible actions that will drive their organization towards greater efficiency and success.

In the days that follow, the document becomes a central tool in their strategy meetings and implementation plans. It guides their efforts, keeps them focused, and serves as a benchmark for their progress. With this comprehensive blueprint, they are well-equipped to navigate the challenges ahead and achieve their goal of sustainable success.

3

Chapter 3: Designing Effective Systems

Streamlining Recruitment Processes

With the blueprint for the new system taking shape, Alex and Sarah turn their attention to the first subpoint: streamlining recruitment processes. Recognizing that hiring top talent is crucial to the department's success, they set out to revamp the recruitment process from start to finish.

Gathered around a conference table littered with resumes and job descriptions, Alex and Sarah brainstorm ideas for optimizing each step of the recruitment journey. They discuss ways to attract a wider pool of candidates, streamline the screening process, and expedite the interview and selection process.

As they dive deeper into their discussion, Alex feels a sense of excitement building within him. This is their chance to redefine the way the HR department recruits new talent, to build a process that is not only efficient but also effective in identifying the best candidates for the job.

But streamlining recruitment processes is no easy task. With so many variables to consider, Alex finds himself grappling with uncertainty and doubt. How can they possibly create a system that balances speed and quality in the hiring process?

Yet Sarah remains calm and focused, her strategic thinking and industry expertise a source of inspiration in the face of adversity. With her guidance, Alex learns to focus on the key priorities, identifying opportunities for improvement and innovation that will drive success.

Together, they sketch out the blueprint for their new recruitment process, mapping out each step in the journey and defining clear roles and responsibilities for everyone involved. They debate the merits of each idea, weighing the pros and cons before reaching a consensus on the best way forward.

As they finalize their plan and prepare to implement it, Alex feels a sense of pride wash over him. By streamlining recruitment processes, they are laying the foundation for a more efficient and successful department, one that is poised to attract and retain top talent in the industry.

As they wrap up their discussion and make plans to begin implementing their new recruitment process, Alex feels a renewed sense of purpose and determination. With Sarah by his side and the support of their colleagues, he knows that they are well-equipped to achieve their goals. Together, they will build an efficient blueprint for success, one recruitment process at a time.

Enhancing Employee Onboarding Procedures

With the recruitment process streamlined, Alex and Sarah shift their focus to the next subpoint: enhancing employee onboarding procedures. Recognizing that a strong onboarding process is essential for setting new hires up for success, they set out to revamp the onboarding experience from day one.

Gathering in a conference room adorned with welcome banners and orientation materials, Alex and Sarah brainstorm ideas for creating a more seamless and impactful onboarding process. They discuss ways to improve communication with new hires, provide clearer guidance on company policies and procedures, and foster a sense of belonging and engagement from the outset.

As they delve deeper into their discussion, Alex feels a sense of anticipation building within him. This is their chance to redefine the way the HR department welcomes new employees, to build an onboarding process that not only accelerates integration but also sets the stage for long-term success.

But enhancing employee onboarding procedures is no small feat. With so many moving parts to consider, Alex finds himself grappling with uncertainty and doubt. How can they possibly create a process that addresses the diverse needs and expectations of new hires?

Yet Sarah remains focused and determined, her empathy and insight a source of inspiration in the face of adversity. With her guidance, Alex learns to prioritize the key elements of the onboarding experience, identifying opportunities for improvement and innovation that will make a real difference.

Together, they sketch out the blueprint for their new onboarding process, mapping out each step in the journey and defining clear objectives and milestones along the way. They debate the merits of each idea, drawing from their own experiences as new hires and feedback from current employees.

As they finalize their plan and prepare to roll it out, Alex feels a sense of pride wash over him. By enhancing employee onboarding procedures, they are laying the foundation for a more engaged and productive workforce, one that is poised to thrive in the company's culture.

As they wrap up their discussion and make plans to begin implementing their new onboarding process, Alex feels a renewed sense of purpose and determination. With Sarah by his side and the support of their colleagues, he knows that they are well-equipped to achieve their goals. Together, they will build an efficient blueprint for success, one new hire at a time.

Defining Objectives and Goals for Efficiency Improvement

With a stack of papers and a whiteboard at their disposal, Alex and Sarah embark on the crucial task of defining objectives and goals for efficiency improvement within the HR department. They recognize that without clear targets to aim for, their efforts could easily veer off course.

As they settle into their seats, Alex feels a surge of anticipation coursing through him. This is their chance to establish a roadmap for success, to set ambitious yet achievable goals that will guide their efforts towards greater efficiency and effectiveness.

But defining objectives and goals is no simple task. With so many factors to consider, Alex finds himself grappling with uncertainty and doubt. How can they possibly create a set of goals that captures the complexity of their department's operations?

Yet Sarah remains calm and focused, her strategic thinking and analytical skills a beacon of clarity in the fog of uncertainty. With her guidance, Alex learns to focus on the core priorities, identifying key areas for improvement and setting realistic targets that align with the department's overarching goals.

Together, they brainstorm ideas for objectives and goals, drawing from their own experiences and insights gained from their analysis of current processes. They debate the merits of each idea, weighing the potential benefits against the practical constraints of implementation.

As they delve deeper into their discussion, Alex feels a sense of clarity begin to emerge. By defining objectives and goals for efficiency improvement, they are laying the groundwork for a more focused and purpose-driven approach to their work.

But as they finalize their list of objectives and goals, they also encounter challenges. Some goals seem overly ambitious, while others may not go far enough in driving meaningful change.

Yet Sarah remains undeterred, her unwavering optimism a source of inspiration in the face of adversity. With her support, Alex finds the courage to push forward, confident in their ability to overcome any obstacles that stand in their way.

As they wrap up their discussion and prepare to present their objectives and goals to the rest of the team, Alex feels a renewed sense of purpose and determination. With Sarah by his side and the support of their colleagues, he knows that they are well-equipped to achieve their goals. Together, they will build an efficient blueprint for success, one objective at a time.

Design Thinking Principles for System Design

As the sun casts long shadows through the office windows, Alex and Sarah shift their focus to the next subpoint: applying design thinking principles for system design. Recognizing that a human-centered approach is essential for creating systems that truly meet the needs of the department, they set out to infuse their blueprint with creativity and empathy.

Gathering around a whiteboard adorned with colorful sticky notes and markers, Alex and Sarah dive into a lively discussion on the principles of design thinking. They explore concepts such as empathy, ideation, prototyping, and iteration, seeking to harness the power of human-centered design to drive innovation and efficiency.

As they delve deeper into their discussion, Alex feels a sense of excitement building within him. This is their chance to reimagine the way the HR department operates, to build systems that are not only efficient but also intuitive and user-friendly for everyone involved.

But applying design thinking principles is no small feat. With so many perspectives to consider, Alex finds himself grappling with uncertainty and doubt. How can they possibly create systems that cater to the diverse needs and preferences of their team members?

Yet Sarah remains steadfast, her creativity and ingenuity a source of inspiration in the face of adversity. With her guidance, Alex learns to embrace the principles of design thinking, approaching each challenge with an open mind and a willingness to iterate and innovate.

Together, they sketch out the blueprint for their new systems, incorporating elements of design thinking at every step of the process. They brainstorm ideas for user personas, empathy maps, and journey maps, seeking to gain a deeper understanding of the needs and pain points of their team members.

As they finalize their designs and prepare to prototype their new systems, Alex feels a sense of pride wash over him. By applying design thinking principles, they are laying the foundation for a more human-centered approach to their work, one that puts the needs of their team members front and center.

As they wrap up their discussion and make plans to begin prototyping, Alex feels a renewed sense of purpose and determination. With Sarah by his side and the support of their colleagues, he knows that they are well-equipped to achieve their goals. Together, they will build an efficient blueprint for success, one design thinking principle at a time.

Mapping Out Workflows and Processes

Feeling invigorated by their exploration of design thinking principles, Alex and Sarah decide to take their brainstorming sessions to different locations to inspire fresh perspectives. Their first stop: a cozy café nestled in the heart of the city.

As they settle into a corner booth, surrounded by the aroma of freshly brewed coffee and the gentle hum of conversation, Alex and Sarah begin to map out workflows and processes for the HR department's new systems.

With laptops open and notebooks at the ready, they dive into their discussion, sketching out diagrams and flowcharts on the café's napkins and tablecloths. Each stroke of the pen brings them closer to a deeper understanding of how their new systems will function, how tasks will flow seamlessly from one stage to the next.

As they work, Alex feels a sense of liberation wash over him. Breaking free from the confines of the office has sparked his creativity, opening his mind to new possibilities and ideas that he hadn't considered before.

But mapping out workflows and processes is no easy task. With so many intricacies to consider, Alex finds himself grappling with uncertainty and doubt. How can they possibly capture the complexity of the department's operations in a few simple diagrams?

Yet Sarah remains calm and focused, her strategic thinking and attention to detail a source of reassurance in the face of uncertainty. With her guidance, Alex learns to break down complex processes into manageable chunks, identifying key stages and decision points that will drive efficiency and effectiveness.

Together, they sketch out the blueprint for their new workflows, mapping out each step in the process and defining clear roles and responsibilities for everyone involved. They brainstorm ideas for optimizing each stage, seeking to eliminate bottlenecks and streamline operations wherever possible.

As they wrap up their discussion and prepare to leave the café, Alex feels a sense of satisfaction wash over him. By mapping out workflows and processes in a new environment, they have gained fresh insights and perspectives that will inform their approach moving forward.

As they make plans to continue their meetings in different locations, Alex feels a renewed sense of excitement for the journey ahead. With Sarah by his side and the support of their colleagues, he knows that they are well-equipped to achieve their goals. Together, they will build an efficient blueprint for success, one workflow at a time.

Integrating Technology for Automation and Optimization

In the bustling tech lab of their company's innovation center, Alex and Sarah are joined by two key team members, Marcus, a software developer, and Grace, a process engineer. They gather around a sleek conference table, laptops and tablets at the ready, to discuss the next critical step in their efficiency journey: integrating technology for automation and optimization.

The room buzzes with excitement as Marcus sets up a demo on the main screen. "Today, we're going to explore how automation can revolutionize our workflows and processes," he begins, his enthusiasm infectious. "With the right technology, we can eliminate repetitive tasks, reduce errors, and free up time for more strategic activities."

Sarah, always the visionary, nods in agreement. "Automation is not just about replacing manual work. It's about enhancing our capabilities and enabling us to achieve more with less effort. It's about optimizing our operations to be more agile and responsive to change."

Grace, who has a keen eye for detail, chimes in. "We need to carefully map out our processes to identify the best areas for automation. It's crucial to ensure that the technology we implement aligns with our goals and integrates seamlessly with our existing systems."

Alex, absorbing their insights, feels a surge of determination. "Let's start by identifying the key processes that would benefit most from automation," he suggests. "Once we have a clear picture, we can work with Marcus to develop and implement the right technological solutions."

As they delve into the discussion, Marcus showcases several

automation tools and platforms that have the potential to transform their operations. From robotic process automation (RPA) to advanced analytics and machine learning, the possibilities seem endless.

"We can start with automating our data entry and reporting processes," Marcus proposes. "This will not only save us time but also ensure greater accuracy and consistency in our data management."

Grace, thinking ahead, adds, "We should also consider implementing workflow automation software to streamline our project management and collaboration efforts. This will help us stay organized and improve communication across teams."

With a clear plan in mind, the team sets to work, mapping out their workflows and identifying pain points that could be addressed through automation. The energy in the room is palpable as they brainstorm, strategize, and innovate together.

Over the next few weeks, they roll out the new technologies, carefully monitoring their impact and making adjustments as needed. The results are immediate and impressive. Tasks that once took hours to complete are now done in minutes. Errors are significantly reduced, and team members find themselves with more time to focus on high-value activities.

As they celebrate their successes, Alex reflects on the journey they've embarked on. By integrating technology for automation and optimization, they've not only improved their efficiency but also set the stage for sustainable growth and innovation.

Standing in the lab, surrounded by his dedicated team, Alex feels a profound sense of accomplishment. With the right tools and a shared commitment to excellence, they have the power to transform their organization and achieve remarkable success.

"We've only just begun," Sarah says, her eyes shining with excitement. "The future is full of possibilities, and with technology on our side, there's no limit to what we can achieve."

As they look ahead to the next phase of their efficiency journey, Alex knows that they are on the right path. Together, they will continue to innovate, optimize, and drive positive change, creating a blueprint for success that will inspire others for years to come.

Establishing Key Performance Indicators (KPIs)

In the modern and spacious boardroom, Alex, Sarah, Marcus, and Grace reconvene, ready to tackle the next crucial step in their efficiency journey: establishing key performance indicators (KPIs). The walls of the room are adorned with large screens displaying data charts and performance metrics, a testament to the company's commitment to transparency and continuous improvement.

"KPIs are our compass," Alex begins, addressing the team with conviction. "They'll guide us, tell us where we are, and show us the way forward. We need to establish clear, measurable indicators that align with our strategic goals."

Sarah nods, adding, "KPIs need to be specific and actionable. They should reflect both our short-term objectives and our long-term vision. We must ensure everyone understands their importance and how they contribute to our overall success."

Marcus, ever the data enthusiast, pulls up a presentation on the main screen. "Let's start by identifying the areas we want to measure. We need to cover all critical aspects: financial performance, operational efficiency, customer satisfaction, and employee engagement."

Grace, with her analytical mind, suggests, "For financial performance, we can look at metrics like revenue growth, profit margins, and cost reduction. These will give us a clear picture of our financial health."

Marcus nods in agreement. "For operational efficiency, we can track production cycle times, error rates, and downtime. These KPIs will help us identify bottlenecks and areas for improvement."

As the discussion progresses, they meticulously outline KPIs for each area. They decide on customer satisfaction metrics such as Net Promoter Score (NPS) and customer retention rates, while employee engagement will be measured through surveys, turnover rates, and productivity metrics.

Sarah emphasizes the importance of regular review. "KPIs are not static. We need to review them regularly, adjust our strategies as needed, and ensure they remain aligned with our goals."

To bring their KPIs to life, they decide to implement a dashboard system that provides real-time visibility into their performance metrics. Marcus volunteers to spearhead the development of this system, ensuring that the data is accurate, accessible, and user-friendly.

Over the following weeks, the team works diligently to set up the dashboard and communicate the new KPIs to the entire organization. They hold training sessions to explain the importance of KPIs and how they will be used to drive improvement.

One sunny afternoon, the team gathers again in the boardroom to see the live dashboard in action for the first time. The screens light up with colorful graphs and charts, depicting various KPIs in real-time. There's a palpable sense of accomplishment and anticipation in the room.

"This is incredible," Grace remarks, her eyes fixed on the dashboard. "We can see exactly where we stand and where we need to focus our efforts."

Alex feels a surge of pride. "This is just the beginning. With these KPIs, we have a clear roadmap to guide us. We'll use this data to make informed decisions, drive continuous improvement, and achieve sustainable success."

As they conclude their meeting, Alex takes a moment to address the team. "By establishing these KPIs, we've laid a strong foundation for our efficiency journey. But remember, it's not just about the numbers. It's about what we do with them. Let's stay committed, stay focused, and continue to strive for excellence."

The team disperses, each member filled with a renewed sense of purpose and determination. They know that the path ahead will be challenging, but with clear KPIs and a shared vision, they are ready to navigate it together, driving their organization towards a future of unparalleled efficiency and sustainable success.

Building Flexibility and Scalability into Systems

The company's innovation center is buzzing with activity as Alex, Sarah, Marcus, and Grace gather for yet another pivotal discussion. This time, they've invited two more colleagues to join them: Ravi, a senior systems architect, and Lily, a strategic planner. The topic of the day is building flexibility and scalability into their systems—an essential step to ensure their efficiency efforts can grow and adapt over time.

They settle into a cozy corner of the tech lab, where whiteboards are filled with complex diagrams and sticky notes. Alex kicks off the meeting. "We've laid down the groundwork with our KPIs, but to truly thrive, our systems need to be both flexible and scalable. We need to ensure they can adapt to changes and grow as we do."

Ravi, with his extensive background in systems architecture, takes the lead. "Flexibility means designing systems that can handle variability and change without significant rework. Scalability is about ensuring those systems can grow in capacity without a loss of performance."

Lily chimes in, "We need to consider future growth and potential market shifts. If we build scalability into our systems now, we won't be caught off guard when our operations expand or our environment changes."

Sarah nods thoughtfully. "Agility is key. Our processes should be able to pivot quickly in response to new opportunities or challenges. But how do we practically achieve this?"

Marcus, ever the tech enthusiast, pulls up a digital model on his tablet. "One way is through modular system design. By creating systems in modular components, we can easily upgrade or replace parts without overhauling the entire system."

Ravi elaborates, "Think of it like building blocks. Each module can be developed, tested, and improved independently. This approach not only supports flexibility but also makes scaling up much easier."

Grace, always focused on practical implementation, suggests, "We should also incorporate cloud-based solutions. They offer the scalability we need, as we can easily adjust our storage and computing power based on demand."

Lily adds, "From a strategic perspective, we should create a

CHAPTER 3: DESIGNING EFFECTIVE SYSTEMS

roadmap that anticipates different growth scenarios. This will help us plan and allocate resources more effectively."

As they dive deeper into the discussion, the team brainstorms specific strategies. They decide to adopt a microservices architecture for their software systems, allowing different parts of their applications to be developed and scaled independently. They also plan to invest in cloud infrastructure to support dynamic scaling of their operations.

Marcus presents a prototype of their new system architecture. "This design ensures that as we grow, we can scale each component independently. It's a game-changer for our agility."

Ravi points out, "We also need to ensure that our team is trained to handle these flexible systems. Continuous learning and adaptability will be crucial."

As they map out their plan, Alex feels a sense of excitement. "We're not just building systems for today; we're building for the future. Flexibility and scalability will be our competitive advantage."

The weeks that follow are filled with intense collaboration. The team works tirelessly to implement their new modular systems and transition their operations to the cloud. They conduct training sessions to ensure everyone understands the new architecture and how to leverage its flexibility.

One sunny afternoon, the team gathers in a new location: a vibrant co-working space downtown that Alex chose to inspire creativity and fresh thinking. They review their progress, and the results are promising. Their systems are more adaptable, and their capacity to handle growth has significantly improved.

Sarah looks around the table, her face reflecting the pride and satisfaction they all feel. "We've come a long way, and our systems are now built to last. We're ready to take on whatever the future holds."

Alex stands, raising a cup of coffee in a toast. "To flexibility, scalability, and sustainable success. Together, we've built a foundation that will support our growth and innovation for years to come."

As they clink their cups, the team is filled with a renewed sense of purpose. They know that with their newly flexible and scalable systems, they are well-equipped to navigate the challenges ahead and seize the opportunities that come their way, driving their organization towards a future of unparalleled efficiency and success.

4

Chapter 4: Implementing Efficient Practices

Rolling Out New Technology Solutions

With the overarching goal of implementing efficient practices firmly in mind, Alex and Sarah zero in on the first subpoint: rolling out new technology solutions within the HR department. Recognizing the potential for technology to streamline processes and boost productivity, they set out to introduce innovative solutions that will revolutionize the way their team operates.

Gathered in a conference room adorned with posters of cutting-edge software and sleek gadgets, Alex and Sarah delve into the details of their technology rollout plan. With laptops open and PowerPoint slides at the ready, they begin to outline the steps required to introduce new tools and systems to their team.

As they discuss the benefits and capabilities of each technology solution, Alex feels a sense of excitement building within him. This is their chance to leverage the power of technology to drive efficiency and effectiveness within the HR department, to empower their team members with tools that will enable them to do their best work.

But rolling out new technology solutions is no small feat. With so many moving parts to consider, Alex finds himself grappling with uncertainty and doubt. How can they ensure a smooth transition without disrupting the day-to-day operations of the department?

Yet Sarah remains calm and focused, her strategic thinking and attention to detail a source of reassurance in the face of uncertainty. With her guidance, Alex learns to break down the rollout process into manageable steps, identifying key milestones and timelines that will keep their implementation efforts on track.

Together, they develop a comprehensive rollout plan that includes training sessions, support resources, and feedback mechanisms to ensure that their team members feel comfortable and confident using the new technology solutions. They anticipate potential challenges and develop contingency plans to address them proactively, minimizing disruptions and maximizing success.

As they finalize their rollout plan and prepare to begin implementation, Alex feels a sense of pride wash over him. By introducing new technology solutions, they are laying the foundation for a more efficient and effective HR department, one that is better equipped to meet the needs of their team members and the organization as a whole.

As they wrap up their discussion and make plans to kick off the rollout process, Alex feels a renewed sense of purpose and determination. With Sarah by his side and the support of their colleagues, he knows that they are well-equipped to achieve their goals. Together, they will continue to build an efficient blueprint for success, one technology solution at a time.

Creating a Roadmap for Implementation

With the ambitious goal of rolling out new technology solutions within the HR department, Alex and Sarah recognize the importance of creating a roadmap for implementation. They understand that a well-defined plan will be critical to ensure a smooth transition and successful adoption of the new tools and systems.

Seated at a large conference table, surrounded by charts and diagrams, Alex and Sarah dive into the task of creating a comprehensive roadmap. With markers in hand, they sketch out timelines, milestones, and key deliverables, mapping out the journey ahead in vivid detail.

As they brainstorm ideas and debate the best approach, Alex feels a sense of excitement building within him. This is their chance to chart a course towards a more efficient and effective HR department, one that harnesses the power of technology to drive innovation and productivity.

But creating a roadmap for implementation is no small feat. With so many moving parts to consider, Alex finds himself grappling with uncertainty and doubt. How can they possibly account for every contingency and ensure that their plan is foolproof?

Yet Sarah remains calm and focused, her strategic thinking and attention to detail a source of reassurance in the face of uncertainty. With her guidance, Alex learns to break down the implementation process into manageable phases, identifying key activities and dependencies that will shape their roadmap.

Together, they develop a comprehensive timeline that spans several months, with clear milestones and checkpoints along the way. They allocate resources and assign responsibilities to ensure that everyone is aligned and working towards the same goals.

As they finalize their roadmap and prepare to present it to the rest of the team, Alex feels a sense of pride wash over him. By creating a roadmap for implementation, they are laying the foundation for a successful rollout of new technology solutions, one that will transform the way the HR department operates for years to come.

As they wrap up their discussion and make plans to begin execution, Alex feels a renewed sense of purpose and determination. With Sarah by his side and the support of their colleagues, he knows that they are well-equipped to achieve their goals. Together, they will continue to build an efficient blueprint for success, one step at a time.

Prioritizing Improvements Based on Impact and Feasibility

With the roadmap for technology implementation in hand, Alex and Sarah turn their attention to the critical task of prioritizing improvements based on impact and feasibility. They understand that not all changes can be implemented at once, and it's essential to focus on the initiatives that will deliver the most significant benefits with the resources available.

Seated in a conference room adorned with charts and graphs, Alex and Sarah immerse themselves in the process of evaluating potential improvements. They pore over data and analyze feedback from team members, seeking to identify opportunities for optimization and enhancement.

As they delve deeper into their analysis, Alex feels a sense of urgency building within him. This is their chance to make a real difference in the efficiency and effectiveness of the HR department, to prioritize initiatives that will have a tangible impact on their team's success.

But prioritizing improvements is no easy task. With limited resources and competing priorities, Alex finds himself grappling with uncertainty and doubt. How can they possibly determine which initiatives to pursue first?

Yet Sarah remains calm and focused, her strategic thinking and analytical skills a source of reassurance in the face of adversity. With her guidance, Alex learns to prioritize improvements based on their potential impact on the department's operations and their feasibility given the available resources and constraints.

Together, they develop a framework for evaluating potential improvements, assigning each initiative a score based on criteria such as projected benefits, resource requirements, and alignment with strategic goals. They debate the merits of each initiative, weighing the potential risks and rewards before reaching a consensus on the priorities for implementation.

As they finalize their list of prioritized improvements, Alex feels a sense of pride wash over him. By focusing their efforts on initiatives with the greatest potential for impact and feasibility, they are laying the groundwork for a more efficient and effective HR department, one that is better equipped to meet the needs of their team members and the organization as a whole.

As they wrap up their discussion and make plans to begin

implementation, Alex feels a renewed sense of purpose and determination. With Sarah by his side and the support of their colleagues, he knows that they are well-equipped to achieve their goals. Together, they will continue to build an efficient blueprint for success, one prioritized improvement at a time.

Developing Change Management Strategies

With their priorities for improvement identified and their roadmap for implementation laid out, Alex and Sarah shift their focus to the next crucial subpoint: developing change management strategies. Recognizing that successful implementation relies on effective change management, they set out to ensure that their team is prepared and empowered to embrace the upcoming changes.

Deciding to break away from the confines of the office, Alex and Sarah opt to hold their change management strategy sessions in different localities, seeking inspiration from new environments. Their first destination: a serene park nestled in the heart of the city.

As they find a shaded spot beneath a towering oak tree, Alex and Sarah spread out their notes and begin to brainstorm ideas for managing change within the HR department. With the tranquil surroundings inspiring creativity, they delve into the complexities of change management, exploring strategies to mitigate resistance and foster a culture of adaptability.

As they discuss the importance of communication, training, and stakeholder engagement, Alex feels a sense of urgency building within him. This is their chance to lay the groundwork for a successful implementation, to ensure that their team members are prepared and motivated to embrace the changes ahead.

But developing change management strategies is no easy task. With so many variables to consider, Alex finds himself grappling with uncertainty and doubt. How can they possibly anticipate and address the diverse reactions and challenges that may arise during the implementation process?

Yet Sarah remains calm and focused, her strategic thinking and empathy a source of reassurance in the face of uncertainty. With her guidance, Alex learns to approach change management with empathy and understanding, recognizing the importance of addressing the emotional aspects of change as well as the practical considerations.

Together, they sketch out a comprehensive change management plan that includes clear communication channels, targeted training programs, and opportunities for feedback and engagement. They brainstorm ideas for overcoming resistance and fostering a sense of ownership and buy-in among their team members.

As they finalize their change management plan and prepare to roll it out, Alex feels a sense of pride wash over him. By developing effective change management strategies, they are laying the foundation for a smooth and successful implementation, one that will position the HR department for long-term success.

As they wrap up their discussion and make plans to begin executing their change management plan, Alex feels a renewed sense of purpose and determination. With Sarah by his side and the support of their colleagues, he knows that they are well-equipped to navigate the challenges of change and emerge stronger on the other side. Together, they will continue to build an efficient blueprint for success, one change management strategy at a time.

Training Staff on New Processes and Tools

With their change management strategies in place, Alex and Sarah shift their focus to the crucial task of training staff on the new processes and tools that will be introduced as part of the implementation plan. Recognizing that effective training is essential for ensuring a smooth transition, they set out to empower their team members with the knowledge and skills they need to succeed.

Deciding to break away from the traditional office setting once again, Alex and Sarah choose a vibrant co-working space as the venue for their training sessions. Surrounded by the buzz of productivity and innovation, they gather their team members and dive into the intricacies of the new processes and tools.

As they guide their colleagues through hands-on demonstrations and interactive workshops, Alex feels a sense of fulfillment wash over him. This is their chance to equip their team members with the tools they need to thrive in the new environment, to foster a culture of continuous learning and growth within the HR department.

But training staff on new processes and tools is no easy task. With so much information to convey and so many skills to master, Alex finds himself grappling with uncertainty and doubt. How can they possibly ensure that everyone receives the training they need to succeed?

Yet Sarah remains calm and focused, her patience and empathy a source of reassurance in the face of uncertainty. With her guidance, Alex learns to tailor the training sessions to meet the diverse needs and learning styles of their team members, incorporating a mix of lectures, demonstrations, and hands-on activities to keep everyone engaged and motivated.

Together, they work tirelessly to ensure that no stone is left unturned in their training efforts, addressing questions and concerns with care and attention to detail. They provide additional resources and support to those who need it, empowering their team members to take ownership of their learning and development.

As they wrap up their training sessions and reflect on their achievements, Alex feels a sense of pride wash over him. By investing in the training and development of their team members, they are laying the foundation for a more skilled and capable workforce, one that is better equipped to navigate the challenges of the future.

As they make plans to continue their training efforts in the weeks and months ahead, Alex feels a renewed sense of purpose and determination. With Sarah by his side and the support of their colleagues, he knows that they are well-equipped to achieve their goals. Together, they will continue to build an efficient blueprint for success, one training session at a time.

Monitoring Progress and Making Adjustments as Needed

As the implementation of new processes and tools unfolds, Alex and Sarah understand the importance of closely monitoring progress and making adjustments as needed. They recognize that flexibility and adaptability are key to ensuring the success of their efforts, and they are committed to staying vigilant as they navigate the implementation phase.

Choosing to meet in a collaborative workspace overlooking the city skyline, Alex and Sarah gather their team members to discuss progress and assess how the changes are being received. Surrounded by the energy of the bustling city below, they dive into a discussion on monitoring progress and making adjustments as needed.

As they review key performance indicators and metrics, Alex feels a sense of anticipation building within him. This is their chance to evaluate the impact of their efforts and make course corrections as necessary, to ensure that they stay on track towards their goals.

But monitoring progress and making adjustments is no simple task. With so many moving parts to consider, Alex finds himself grappling with uncertainty and doubt. How can they possibly keep tabs on every aspect of the implementation process and identify areas for improvement?

Yet Sarah remains calm and focused, her analytical skills and attention to detail a source of reassurance in the face of uncertainty. With her guidance, Alex learns to interpret the data and feedback they receive, identifying trends and patterns that offer insights into the effectiveness of their efforts.

Together, they develop a plan for ongoing monitoring and evaluation, scheduling regular check-ins and progress reviews to ensure that they stay informed and proactive in their approach. They establish clear protocols for collecting feedback from team members and stakeholders, inviting open and honest communication about what is working well and where adjustments may be needed.

As they wrap up their discussion and make plans to continue monitoring progress, Alex feels a sense of determination wash over him. By staying vigilant and responsive to feedback, they are laying the groundwork for a successful implementation, one that will drive lasting change and improvement within the HR department.

As they gaze out at the city skyline, Alex feels a renewed sense of optimism for the journey ahead. With Sarah by his side and the support of their colleagues, he knows that they are well-equipped to achieve their goals. Together, they will continue to build an efficient blueprint for success, one adjustment at a time.

Celebrating Successes and Reinforcing the Importance of Efficiency

As the implementation of new processes and tools progresses, Alex and Sarah understand the importance of taking time to celebrate successes and reinforce the importance of efficiency within the HR department. They recognize that recognizing achievements and acknowledging the hard work of their team members will help maintain momentum and motivation throughout the implementation phase.

Choosing to meet in a vibrant rooftop bar overlooking the city lights, Alex and Sarah gather their team members to celebrate the milestones they have achieved thus far. Surrounded by the twinkling lights of the skyline, they raise their glasses in a toast to the progress they have made and the successes they have achieved.

As they reflect on their achievements, Alex feels a sense of pride swelling within him. This is their chance to recognize the dedication and hard work of their team members, to celebrate the progress they have made towards building a more efficient and effective HR department.

But celebrating successes is about more than just patting each other on the back. With so much still to be done, Alex finds himself grappling with uncertainty and doubt. How can they take time to celebrate when there are still challenges to overcome and goals to achieve?

Yet Sarah remains steadfast, her optimism and enthusiasm a source of inspiration in the face of uncertainty. With her guidance, Alex learns to appreciate the importance of celebrating even small victories, recognizing that it is these moments of celebration that help keep morale high and motivation strong.

Together, they raise their glasses in a toast to their achievements, sharing stories and laughter as they reflect on the journey they have embarked upon together. They take time to acknowledge the contributions of each team member, recognizing the unique talents and strengths they bring to the table.

As they wrap up their celebration and make plans to continue their efforts, Alex feels a renewed sense of determination wash over him. By taking time to celebrate successes and reinforce the importance of efficiency, they are laying the foundation for a culture of continuous improvement and success within the HR department.

As they gaze out at the city lights, Alex feels a sense of optimism for the future. With Sarah by his side and the support of their colleagues, he knows that they are well-equipped to achieve their goals. Together, they will continue to build an efficient blueprint for success, one celebration at a time.

5

Chapter 5: Leveraging Technology for Efficiency

Exploring Technological Solutions for Efficiency Improvement

In the heart of the technology hub, surrounded by the buzz of innovation and the hum of computers, Alex and Sarah delve into the exploration of technological solutions for efficiency improvement within the HR department.

As they sift through a plethora of software options and technological innovations displayed on screens around them, Alex feels a surge of excitement. This is their chance to discover the tools that will transform their department, making processes smoother, faster, and more efficient.

But amidst the sea of possibilities, Alex finds himself grappling with uncertainty. How can they navigate this maze of options and choose the right solutions for their needs?

With Sarah's guidance, Alex learns to approach the exploration with a strategic mindset. They carefully evaluate each technology solution, considering factors such as functionality, scalability, and compatibility with existing systems.

As they delve deeper, they uncover a treasure trove of possibilities: applicant tracking systems to streamline recruitment, employee self-service portals to automate administrative tasks, and analytics platforms to gain insights into workforce trends.

Yet, the abundance of options also presents a challenge. With so many technologies to consider, Alex and Sarah must carefully weigh the pros and cons of each, ensuring that they select solutions that will deliver maximum impact with minimal disruption.

Together, they chart a course through the technological landscape, identifying the solutions that align most closely with their goals for efficiency improvement. They engage in spirited debates, weighing the merits of each option and envisioning how it could transform their department for the better.

As they wrap up their exploration, Alex feels a sense of clarity begin to emerge. By carefully evaluating technological solutions for efficiency improvement, they are laying the groundwork for a more streamlined and effective HR department, one that is ready to embrace the future of work with confidence and agility.

As they make plans to begin implementation, Alex feels a renewed sense of purpose and determination. With Sarah by his side and the support of their colleagues, he knows that they are well-equipped to achieve their goals. Together, they will continue to harness the power of technology to drive efficiency and innovation, propelling their department towards even greater success.

Adopting Project Management and Collaboration Tools

With their exploration of technological solutions underway, Alex and Sarah turn their attention to the adoption of project management and collaboration tools. Recognizing the importance of effective communication and coordination in driving efficiency, they set out to find tools that will enable seamless collaboration and streamline project workflows within the HR department.

Seated in a sleek conference room with panoramic views of the city skyline, Alex and Sarah gather their team members to discuss the adoption of project management and collaboration tools. Surrounded by screens displaying the latest software options, they dive into a lively discussion on the merits of each solution.

As they explore the features and capabilities of various tools, Alex feels a sense of anticipation building within him. This is their chance to revolutionize the way their team works, to break down silos and foster a culture of collaboration and transparency.

But adopting project management and collaboration tools is no small feat. With so many options available, Alex finds himself grappling with uncertainty and doubt. How can they choose the right tools that will meet the unique needs of their department and support their goals for efficiency improvement?

Yet Sarah remains calm and focused, her strategic thinking and attention to detail a source of reassurance in the face of uncertainty. With her guidance, Alex learns to approach the adoption process systematically, evaluating each tool based on criteria such as ease of use, scalability, and integration with existing systems.

Together, they narrow down their options and select a suite of project management and collaboration tools that align closely with their goals. They develop a plan for implementation, outlining key milestones and timelines for rolling out the new tools to their team members.

As they finalize their plans and prepare to begin implementation, Alex feels a sense of excitement wash over him. By adopting project management and collaboration tools, they are laying the foundation for a more efficient and cohesive team, one that is better equipped to tackle projects and deliver results with speed and precision.

As they make plans to roll out the new tools and train their team members, Alex feels a renewed sense of purpose and determination. With Sarah by his side and the support of their colleagues, he knows that they are well-equipped to achieve their goals. Together, they will continue to leverage the power of technology to drive efficiency and innovation within the HR department, propelling their team towards even greater success.

Implementing Workflow Automation Software

As the discussions about technological solutions continue, Alex and Sarah shift their focus to the implementation of workflow automation software. Recognizing the potential of automation to streamline repetitive tasks and enhance efficiency, they are determined to introduce these tools into their department.

Seated in a modern office space equipped with cutting-edge technology, Alex and Sarah gather their team members to discuss the implementation of workflow automation software.

CHAPTER 5: LEVERAGING TECHNOLOGY FOR EFFICIENCY

Surrounded by screens displaying demonstrations of the latest automation tools, they dive into the details of how these solutions can revolutionize their workflows.

As they explore the features and functionalities of various automation software options, Alex feels a sense of excitement building within him. This is their opportunity to eliminate manual processes, reduce errors, and free up valuable time for more strategic tasks.

But implementing workflow automation software is no small undertaking. With so many complexities to consider, Alex finds himself grappling with uncertainty and doubt. How can they ensure a smooth transition without disrupting the day-to-day operations of the department?

Yet Sarah remains composed and focused, her strategic thinking and problem-solving skills a source of reassurance in the face of uncertainty. With her guidance, Alex learns to approach the implementation process systematically, breaking it down into manageable steps and anticipating potential challenges.

Together, they develop a comprehensive implementation plan that includes thorough testing, training sessions for team members, and a phased rollout to minimize disruption. They collaborate closely with IT experts to ensure seamless integration with existing systems and processes.

As they finalize their plans and prepare to begin implementation, Alex feels a sense of determination wash over him. By implementing workflow automation software, they are laying the groundwork for a more efficient and streamlined HR department, one that is better equipped to meet the needs of their team members and the organization as a whole.

As they make plans to roll out the new software and provide

support to their team members, Alex feels a renewed sense of purpose and confidence. With Sarah by his side and the support of their colleagues, he knows that they are well-equipped to achieve their goals. Together, they will continue to harness the power of technology to drive efficiency and innovation within the HR department, propelling their team towards even greater success.

Utilizing Data Analytics for Insights and Decision-Making

In a sleek, modern boardroom with floor-to-ceiling windows offering panoramic views of the cityscape, Alex and Sarah gather their team members to explore the realm of data analytics for insights and decision-making. Surrounded by screens displaying intricate charts and graphs, they embark on a journey to harness the power of data to drive efficiency and inform strategic decisions within the HR department.

As they delve into the intricacies of data analytics, Alex feels a sense of anticipation building within him. This is their opportunity to unlock valuable insights hidden within the vast troves of data at their disposal, to gain a deeper understanding of their operations and make informed decisions that propel their department forward.

But diving into data analytics is no small feat. With so much information to sift through and analyze, Alex finds himself grappling with uncertainty and doubt. How can they make sense of the data overload and extract meaningful insights that drive actionable outcomes?

Yet Sarah remains composed and focused, her analytical skills and strategic mindset a source of reassurance in the face of uncertainty. With her guidance, Alex learns to approach data analytics systematically, identifying key metrics and performance indicators that align with their goals for efficiency improvement.

Together, they explore a range of analytics tools and techniques, from descriptive analytics that provide insights into past performance to predictive analytics that forecast future trends. They collaborate closely with data scientists and analysts to develop customized dashboards and reports that provide real-time visibility into their department's operations.

As they dive deeper into the data, Alex feels a sense of clarity begin to emerge. By utilizing data analytics for insights and decision-making, they are gaining a competitive edge, leveraging data-driven insights to drive efficiency, and make informed decisions that propel their department forward.

As they make plans to continue their exploration of data analytics, Alex feels a renewed sense of purpose and determination. With Sarah by his side and the support of their colleagues, he knows that they are well-equipped to harness the power of data to drive efficiency and innovation within the HR department, propelling their team towards even greater success.

Integrating Cloud Computing for Scalability and Accessibility

In a dynamic co-working space adorned with sleek, minimalist decor and buzzing with creative energy, Alex and Sarah convene their team members to discuss the integration of cloud computing for scalability and accessibility within the HR department. Surrounded by the innovative atmosphere of the space, they delve into the possibilities of leveraging cloud technology to transform their operations.

As they explore the concept of cloud computing, Alex feels a sense of excitement building within him. This is their chance to break free from the limitations of traditional IT infrastructure, to embrace a flexible and scalable approach to managing their data and applications.

But integrating cloud computing is no simple task. With so many considerations to take into account, Alex finds himself grappling with uncertainty and doubt. How can they ensure a seamless transition to the cloud without sacrificing security or reliability?

Yet Sarah remains calm and focused, her strategic thinking and technical expertise a source of reassurance in the face of uncertainty. With her guidance, Alex learns to approach the integration process systematically, identifying the key workloads and applications that are best suited for migration to the cloud.

Together, they develop a comprehensive plan for integrating cloud computing into their operations. They collaborate closely with cloud service providers to ensure that their data is secure and compliant with regulatory requirements, while also optimizing performance and cost-effectiveness.

As they finalize their plans and prepare to begin implementation, Alex feels a sense of anticipation wash over him. By integrating cloud computing for scalability and accessibility, they are laying the foundation for a more agile and responsive HR department, one that is ready to adapt to the evolving needs of the organization.

As they make plans to migrate their data and applications to the cloud, Alex feels a renewed sense of purpose and determination. With Sarah by his side and the support of their colleagues, he knows that they are well-equipped to achieve their goals. Together, they will continue to leverage the power of technology to drive efficiency and innovation within the HR department, propelling their team towards even greater success.

Ensuring Cybersecurity Measures are in Place

In a secure conference room with opaque walls and encrypted communication lines, Alex and Sarah convene their team members to discuss the critical importance of ensuring cybersecurity measures are in place as they integrate new technologies into the HR department. Surrounded by screens displaying intricate security protocols and threat assessments, they dive into the complexities of safeguarding their digital assets.

As they explore the intricacies of cybersecurity, Alex feels a sense of gravity settle over the room. This is their opportunity to protect sensitive data and ensure the integrity of their systems against potential threats, both internal and external.

But ensuring cybersecurity measures are in place is no small task. With cyber threats evolving constantly, Alex finds himself grappling with uncertainty and doubt. How can they stay one step ahead of hackers and cybercriminals who are constantly looking for vulnerabilities to exploit?

Yet Sarah remains composed and focused, her expertise in cybersecurity a source of reassurance in the face of uncertainty. With her guidance, Alex learns to approach cybersecurity systematically, identifying potential risks and implementing robust measures to mitigate them.

Together, they develop a comprehensive cybersecurity plan that includes encryption protocols, multi-factor authentication, and regular security audits. They collaborate closely with IT security experts to ensure that their systems are fortified against unauthorized access and data breaches.

As they finalize their plans and prepare to implement their cybersecurity measures, Alex feels a sense of urgency wash over him. By ensuring cybersecurity measures are in place, they are protecting their department and the organization as a whole from potential threats that could compromise their operations and reputation.

As they make plans to train their team members on cybersecurity best practices and conduct regular security awareness campaigns, Alex feels a renewed sense of purpose and determination. With Sarah by his side and the support of their colleagues, he knows that they are well-equipped to achieve their goals. Together, they will continue to prioritize security and safeguard the digital assets of the HR department, ensuring its resilience and success in the face of cyber threats.

6

Chapter 6: Cultivating a Culture of Efficiency

Fostering a Mindset of Continuous Improvement

In the heart of their department's collaborative workspace, Alex and Sarah gather their team members to discuss the crucial subpoint of fostering a mindset of continuous improvement. Surrounded by whiteboards adorned with brainstorming notes and colorful sticky notes, they delve into the importance of embracing change and innovation as a fundamental part of their culture.

As they begin the discussion, Alex feels a surge of determination. This is their opportunity to instill a sense of curiosity and adaptability within their team, to create an environment where every idea is valued and every challenge is seen as an opportunity for growth.

But fostering a mindset of continuous improvement is no easy task. With entrenched habits and resistance to change to overcome, Alex finds himself grappling with uncertainty and doubt. How can they inspire their team members to embrace a culture of continuous learning and growth?

Yet Sarah remains steadfast, her belief in the power of continuous improvement as a driver of success unwavering. With her guidance, Alex learns to approach the challenge with creativity and empathy, recognizing that change must come from within each individual.

Together, they develop a multifaceted approach to fostering a mindset of continuous improvement. They launch initiatives such as regular brainstorming sessions, cross-functional collaboration projects, and opportunities for skill development and training.

As they roll out their initiatives and begin to see the first signs of progress, Alex feels a sense of optimism begin to take root. By fostering a mindset of continuous improvement, they are laying the foundation for a department that is not only efficient but also innovative and resilient in the face of change.

As they make plans to continue nurturing a culture of continuous improvement, Alex feels a renewed sense of purpose and determination. With Sarah by his side and the support of their colleagues, he knows that they are well-equipped to achieve their goals. Together, they will continue to inspire their team members to embrace change and strive for excellence, propelling the HR department towards even greater success.

Encouraging Collaboration and Communication

In the heart of their vibrant workspace, Alex and Sarah reconvene their team members to tackle the pivotal subpoint of encouraging collaboration and communication. Surrounded by the buzz of creative energy and the hum of productive conversations, they delve into the importance of fostering open lines of communication and breaking down silos within the department.

As they kick off the discussion, Alex feels a surge of determination. This is their chance to create an environment where every team member feels valued and empowered to contribute their ideas and insights, where collaboration is the norm rather than the exception.

But encouraging collaboration and communication is no small feat. With entrenched departmental boundaries and communication barriers to overcome, Alex finds himself grappling with uncertainty and doubt. How can they create a culture where everyone feels comfortable sharing their thoughts and ideas?

Yet Sarah remains unwavering in her belief that collaboration and communication are the cornerstones of success. With her guidance, Alex learns to approach the challenge with empathy and inclusivity, fostering an environment where everyone's voice is heard and respected.

Together, they develop a multifaceted approach to encouraging collaboration and communication. They introduce initiatives such as regular team meetings, cross-functional project teams, and collaborative brainstorming sessions. They also implement tools and platforms to facilitate communication, such as instant messaging apps and project management software.

As they roll out their initiatives and begin to see the walls between departments crumble, Alex feels a sense of satisfaction wash over him. By encouraging collaboration and communication, they are laying the foundation for a department that is not only efficient but also cohesive and supportive.

As they make plans to continue nurturing a culture of collaboration and communication, Alex feels a renewed sense of purpose and determination. With Sarah by his side and the support of their colleagues, he knows that they are well-equipped to achieve their goals. Together, they will continue to foster an environment where teamwork thrives and innovation flourishes, propelling the HR department towards even greater success.

Recognizing and Rewarding Efficiency Efforts

In the heart of their department's collaborative workspace, Alex and Sarah gather their team members to address the crucial subpoint of recognizing and rewarding efficiency efforts. Surrounded by whiteboards filled with brainstorming ideas and charts mapping progress, they delve into the importance of acknowledging and celebrating the contributions of their team members towards building a culture of efficiency.

As they initiate the discussion, Alex feels a surge of determination. This is their chance to show appreciation for the hard work and dedication of their team members, to create a culture where efficiency is not only valued but also celebrated.

But recognizing and rewarding efficiency efforts is no trivial task. With limited resources and competing priorities to navigate, Alex finds himself grappling with uncertainty and doubt. How can they ensure that their recognition efforts are meaningful and impactful?

Yet Sarah remains steadfast, her belief in the power of recognition as a motivator for continued success unwavering. With her guidance, Alex learns to approach the challenge with creativity and thoughtfulness, recognizing that even small gestures can have a big impact.

Together, they develop a comprehensive plan for recognizing and rewarding efficiency efforts. They launch initiatives such as employee of the month awards, spot bonuses for exceptional performance, and public recognition during team meetings. They also solicit input from team members on other ways they would like to be recognized for their efforts.

As they implement their plan and begin to see the positive effects on morale and motivation, Alex feels a sense of satisfaction wash over him. By recognizing and rewarding efficiency efforts, they are reinforcing the values of their department and inspiring their team members to continue striving for excellence.

As they make plans to continue their recognition efforts and explore new ways to celebrate success, Alex feels a renewed sense of purpose and determination. With Sarah by his side and the support of their colleagues, he knows that they are well-equipped to achieve their goals. Together, they will continue to foster a culture where efficiency is not only expected but also celebrated, propelling the HR department towards even greater success.

Empowering Employees to Take Ownership of Efficiency

In the heart of their collaborative workspace, Alex and Sarah reconvene their team members to tackle the pivotal subpoint of empowering employees to take ownership of efficiency. Surrounded by the energy of innovation and teamwork, they delve into the importance of fostering a sense of ownership and accountability among their team members.

As they kick off the discussion, Alex feels a surge of determination. This is their opportunity to empower their team members to take initiative, to cultivate a sense of pride and ownership in their work, and to become active participants in the quest for efficiency.

But empowering employees to take ownership of efficiency is no small task. With entrenched hierarchies and a fear of failure to overcome, Alex finds himself grappling with uncertainty and doubt. How can they create an environment where every team member feels empowered to contribute their ideas and take ownership of their work?

Yet Sarah remains steadfast, her belief in the power of empowerment as a driver of success unshakeable. With her guidance, Alex learns to approach the challenge with empathy and trust, recognizing that true empowerment comes from within.

Together, they develop a multifaceted approach to empowering employees to take ownership of efficiency. They encourage autonomy and decision-making at all levels, empower team members to lead initiatives and make decisions, and provide opportunities for skill development and growth.

As they roll out their empowerment initiatives and begin to see the transformation in their team members, Alex feels a sense of pride wash over him. By empowering employees to take ownership of efficiency, they are fostering a culture of responsibility and accountability, where every team member feels valued and respected.

As they make plans to continue nurturing a culture of empowerment, Alex feels a renewed sense of purpose and determination. With Sarah by his side and the support of their colleagues, he knows that they are well-equipped to achieve their goals. Together, they will continue to inspire their team members to take ownership of their work and drive the HR department towards even greater success.

Providing Training and Development Opportunities

In the heart of their vibrant workspace, Alex and Sarah reconvene their team members to address the crucial subpoint of providing training and development opportunities. Surrounded by whiteboards filled with plans for growth and innovation, they delve into the importance of investing in their team members' skills and professional development.

As they initiate the discussion, Alex feels a surge of determination. This is their chance to empower their team members to reach their full potential, to provide them with the tools and resources they need to succeed in an ever-evolving work environment.

But providing training and development opportunities is no simple task. With limited resources and competing priorities to navigate, Alex finds himself grappling with uncertainty and doubt. How can they ensure that their training initiatives are effective and impactful?

Yet Sarah remains steadfast, her belief in the power of education and growth as drivers of success unshakeable. With her guidance, Alex learns to approach the challenge with creativity and innovation, recognizing that investing in their team members' development is an investment in the future of the department.

Together, they develop a comprehensive plan for providing training and development opportunities. They launch initiatives such as mentorship programs, workshops, and online courses tailored to the specific needs and interests of their team members. They also provide opportunities for hands-on experience and real-world projects to apply new skills and knowledge.

As they implement their plan and begin to see the transformation in their team members, Alex feels a sense of satisfaction wash over him. By providing training and development opportunities, they are not only equipping their team members with the skills they need to succeed but also fostering a culture of continuous learning and growth.

As they make plans to continue their investment in training and development, Alex feels a renewed sense of purpose and determination. With Sarah by his side and the support of their colleagues, he knows that they are well-equipped to achieve their goals. Together, they will continue to provide their team members with the tools and resources they need to thrive, propelling the HR department towards even greater success.

Leading by Example and Modeling Efficient Behaviors

In the heart of their collaborative workspace, Alex and Sarah reconvene their team members to discuss the pivotal subpoint of leading by example and modeling efficient behaviors. Surrounded by the tangible energy of productivity and teamwork, they delve into the importance of setting the tone for efficiency from the top down.

As they initiate the discussion, Alex feels a surge of determination. This is their opportunity to inspire their team members through their actions, to demonstrate the behaviors and attitudes that they expect from others.

But leading by example and modeling efficient behaviors is

no small feat. With the pressure to perform and the temptation to cut corners, Alex finds himself grappling with uncertainty and doubt. How can they ensure that their actions align with their words and inspire others to follow suit?

Yet Sarah remains steadfast, her belief in the power of leadership as a catalyst for change unshakeable. With her guidance, Alex learns to approach the challenge with authenticity and integrity, recognizing that true leadership is about more than just giving orders – it's about setting an example that others want to follow.

Together, they develop a plan for leading by example and modeling efficient behaviors. They commit to prioritizing their time effectively, minimizing distractions, and making thoughtful decisions that prioritize efficiency and effectiveness. They also pledge to be transparent and accountable in their actions, admitting mistakes and seeking feedback from their team members.

As they begin to implement their plan and lead by example, Alex feels a sense of responsibility wash over him. By modeling efficient behaviors, they are not only setting the standard for their team members but also creating a culture where efficiency is valued and rewarded.

As they make plans to continue leading by example and inspiring others to do the same, Alex feels a renewed sense of purpose and determination. With Sarah by his side and the support of their colleagues, he knows that they are well-equipped to achieve their goals. Together, they will continue to lead with integrity and drive the HR department towards even greater success.

Chapter 7: Measuring and Monitoring Progress

Establishing Metrics for Tracking Efficiency

In the heart of their high-tech meeting room, Alex and Sarah reconvene their team members to tackle the pivotal subpoint of establishing metrics for tracking efficiency. Surrounded by screens displaying complex data visualizations and charts, they dive into the intricacies of defining clear and meaningful metrics to gauge the department's progress towards efficiency goals.

As they initiate the discussion, Alex feels a surge of determination. This is their chance to define the yardsticks by which their success will be measured, to create a roadmap that will guide their efforts and keep them on course towards their objectives.

But establishing metrics for tracking efficiency is no small feat. With numerous factors to consider and differing opinions among team members, Alex finds himself grappling with uncertainty and doubt. How can they ensure that their metrics accurately reflect the department's performance and provide actionable insights for improvement?

Yet Sarah remains steadfast, her expertise in data analysis and performance measurement a beacon of clarity in the midst of uncertainty. With her guidance, Alex learns to approach the challenge with a blend of pragmatism and creativity, recognizing that the key is to strike a balance between simplicity and comprehensiveness.

Together, they engage in a collaborative brainstorming session, drawing on the diverse perspectives and expertise of their team members to identify the most relevant and impactful metrics. They consider factors such as time, cost, quality, and customer satisfaction, striving to create a balanced set of KPIs that capture the department's performance from multiple angles.

As they finalize their list of metrics and prepare to implement them, Alex feels a sense of satisfaction wash over him. By establishing metrics for tracking efficiency, they are not only setting themselves up for success but also creating a culture of accountability and continuous improvement within the department.

As they make plans to monitor their progress and adjust their strategies accordingly, Alex feels a renewed sense of purpose and determination. With Sarah by his side and the support of their colleagues, he knows that they are well-equipped to achieve their goals. Together, they will continue to track their efficiency metrics, identify areas for optimization, and drive the HR department towards even greater success.

Implementing Regular Performance Assessments

In the sleek, modern meeting room, Alex and Sarah reconvene their team to address the critical subpoint of implementing regular performance assessments. Surrounded by screens displaying scheduling software and evaluation templates, they delve into the importance of providing feedback and evaluating individual and team performance.

As they initiate the discussion, Alex feels a surge of determination. This is their chance to create a culture of continuous improvement, where feedback is valued and used to drive growth and development.

But implementing regular performance assessments is no small task. With varying levels of experience and skill among team members, Alex finds himself grappling with uncertainty and doubt. How can they ensure that the assessment process is fair, transparent, and constructive?

Yet Sarah remains steadfast, her expertise in human resource management a guiding light in the sea of uncertainty. With her guidance, Alex learns to approach the challenge with empathy and objectivity, recognizing that performance assessments are not only about evaluating past performance but also about setting goals for the future.

Together, they develop a comprehensive plan for implementing regular performance assessments. They establish clear criteria and benchmarks for evaluation, provide training and support for managers conducting assessments, and create opportunities for feedback and dialogue between team members and their supervisors.

As they roll out their plan and begin to conduct performance assessments, Alex feels a sense of satisfaction wash over him.

By implementing regular performance assessments, they are not only providing valuable feedback to their team members but also fostering a culture of accountability and growth within the department.

As they make plans to review the results of the assessments and set goals for improvement, Alex feels a renewed sense of purpose and determination. With Sarah by his side and the support of their colleagues, he knows that they are well-equipped to achieve their goals. Together, they will continue to assess performance, provide feedback, and drive the HR department towards even greater success.

Implementing Regular Performance Assessments

In the sleek, modern meeting room, Alex and Sarah reconvene their team to address the critical subpoint of implementing regular performance assessments. Surrounded by screens displaying scheduling software and evaluation templates, they delve into the importance of providing feedback and evaluating individual and team performance.

As they initiate the discussion, Alex feels a surge of determination. This is their chance to create a culture of continuous improvement, where feedback is valued and used to drive growth and development.

But implementing regular performance assessments is no small task. With varying levels of experience and skill among team members, Alex finds himself grappling with uncertainty and doubt. How can they ensure that the assessment process is fair, transparent, and constructive?

Yet Sarah remains steadfast, her expertise in human resource management a guiding light in the sea of uncertainty. With her guidance, Alex learns to approach the challenge with empathy and objectivity, recognizing that performance assessments are not only about evaluating past performance but also about setting goals for the future.

Together, they develop a comprehensive plan for implementing regular performance assessments. They establish clear criteria and benchmarks for evaluation, provide training and support for managers conducting assessments, and create opportunities for feedback and dialogue between team members and their supervisors.

As they roll out their plan and begin to conduct performance assessments, Alex feels a sense of satisfaction wash over him. By implementing regular performance assessments, they are not only providing valuable feedback to their team members but also fostering a culture of accountability and growth within the department.

As they make plans to review the results of the assessments and set goals for improvement, Alex feels a renewed sense of purpose and determination. With Sarah by his side and the support of their colleagues, he knows that they are well-equipped to achieve their goals. Together, they will continue to assess performance, provide feedback, and drive the HR department towards even greater success.

Using Feedback Loops to Gather Insights

In the sleek, modern meeting room, Alex and Sarah reconvene their team to address the pivotal subpoint of using feedback loops to gather insights. Surrounded by screens displaying interactive survey tools and feedback collection platforms, they delve into the importance of soliciting input from team members and stakeholders to inform decision-making and drive improvement.

As they initiate the discussion, Alex feels a surge of determination. This is their opportunity to create a culture of openness and transparency, where everyone's voice is heard and valued.

But using feedback loops to gather insights is no small feat. With diverse perspectives and opinions to consider, Alex finds himself grappling with uncertainty and doubt. How can they ensure that the feedback they gather is meaningful and actionable?

Yet Sarah remains steadfast, her expertise in organizational development and employee engagement a beacon of guidance in the face of uncertainty. With her guidance, Alex learns to approach the challenge with humility and curiosity, recognizing that feedback is not only about collecting data but also about fostering a culture of trust and collaboration.

Together, they develop a comprehensive plan for using feedback loops to gather insights. They launch initiatives such as employee surveys, focus groups, and one-on-one feedback sessions to solicit input from team members at all levels. They also establish mechanisms for analyzing and synthesizing the feedback received, identifying common themes and areas for improvement.

As they begin to implement their plan and gather insights from their team members, Alex feels a sense of excitement building within him. By using feedback loops to gather insights, they are not only gaining valuable perspectives on their department's performance but also fostering a culture of continuous improvement and innovation.

As they make plans to review the feedback collected and take action to address any areas of concern, Alex feels a renewed sense of purpose and determination. With Sarah by his side and the support of their colleagues, he knows that they are well-equipped to achieve their goals. Together, they will continue to use feedback loops to gather insights, drive improvement, and propel the HR department towards even greater success.

Conducting Regular Audits of Systems and Processes

In the sleek, modern meeting room, Alex and Sarah reconvene their team to tackle the critical subpoint of conducting regular audits of systems and processes. Surrounded by screens displaying flowcharts of workflows and checklists for audits, they delve into the importance of ensuring that their systems and processes are efficient, effective, and compliant.

As they initiate the discussion, Alex feels a surge of determination. This is their chance to identify areas of inefficiency and opportunity for improvement, to ensure that their department operates at the highest level of performance.

But conducting regular audits of systems and processes is no small task. With complex workflows and myriad regulations to navigate, Alex finds himself grappling with uncertainty and doubt. How can they ensure that their audits are thorough and comprehensive?

Yet Sarah remains steadfast, her expertise in process improvement and compliance a guiding light in the face of uncertainty. With her guidance, Alex learns to approach the challenge with diligence and attention to detail, recognizing that audits are not only about identifying problems but also about finding solutions.

Together, they develop a comprehensive plan for conducting regular audits of systems and processes. They establish clear objectives and criteria for the audits, conduct thorough reviews of documentation and procedures, and engage stakeholders at all levels to gather input and feedback.

As they begin to implement their plan and conduct their audits, Alex feels a sense of anticipation building within him. By conducting regular audits of systems and processes, they are not only ensuring compliance and efficiency but also demonstrating their commitment to excellence and continuous improvement.

As they make plans to review the findings of their audits and implement corrective actions where necessary, Alex feels a renewed sense of purpose and determination. With Sarah by his side and the support of their colleagues, he knows that they are well-equipped to achieve their goals. Together, they will continue to conduct regular audits, drive improvement, and propel the HR department towards even greater success.

Identifying Areas for Further Optimization

In the sleek, modern meeting room, Alex and Sarah reconvene their team to address the critical subpoint of identifying areas for further optimization. Surrounded by screens displaying data dashboards and performance metrics, they delve into the importance of continuously seeking opportunities to improve efficiency and effectiveness within the department.

As they initiate the discussion, Alex feels a surge of determination. This is their chance to uncover hidden inefficiencies and unlock untapped potential, to ensure that their department operates at the peak of performance.

But identifying areas for further optimization is no small feat. With numerous processes and workflows to analyze and countless variables to consider, Alex finds himself grappling with uncertainty and doubt. How can they ensure that they are focusing their efforts on the areas that will yield the greatest return on investment?

Yet Sarah remains steadfast, her expertise in data analysis and process improvement a beacon of guidance in the sea of uncertainty. With her guidance, Alex learns to approach the challenge with a blend of analytical rigor and creativity, recognizing that optimization is not a one-time event but an ongoing process.

Together, they develop a comprehensive plan for identifying areas for further optimization. They leverage data analytics and performance metrics to pinpoint bottlenecks and inefficiencies, conduct root cause analyses to understand the underlying causes, and engage stakeholders to gather input and insights.

As they begin to implement their plan and uncover areas for optimization, Alex feels a sense of excitement building within him. By identifying areas for further optimization, they are not only streamlining their operations but also positioning themselves for long-term success and growth.

As they make plans to implement corrective actions and monitor the impact of their optimization efforts, Alex feels a renewed sense of purpose and determination. With Sarah by his side and the support of their colleagues, he knows that they are well-equipped to achieve their goals. Together, they will continue to identify areas for further optimization, drive improvement, and propel the HR department towards even greater success.

Communicating Progress to Stakeholders

In the sleek, modern meeting room, Alex and Sarah reconvene their team to address the crucial subpoint of communicating progress to stakeholders. Surrounded by screens displaying presentation slides and communication plans, they delve into the importance of transparency and accountability in keeping stakeholders informed about the department's efficiency initiatives.

As they initiate the discussion, Alex feels a surge of determination. This is their chance to build trust and credibility with key stakeholders, to demonstrate the department's commitment to efficiency and continuous improvement.

But communicating progress to stakeholders is no small feat. With diverse stakeholders to consider and complex information to distill, Alex finds himself grappling with uncertainty and doubt. How can they ensure that their communications are clear, concise, and impactful?

Yet Sarah remains steadfast, her expertise in stakeholder management and communication a guiding light in the face of uncertainty. With her guidance, Alex learns to approach the challenge with empathy and strategic thinking, recognizing that effective communication is key to building strong relationships with stakeholders.

Together, they develop a comprehensive communication plan for sharing progress with stakeholders. They identify key messages and objectives, determine the most appropriate channels and formats for communication, and establish regular cadences for updates and reports.

As they begin to implement their plan and communicate progress to stakeholders, Alex feels a sense of satisfaction wash over him. By keeping stakeholders informed and engaged, they are not only demonstrating transparency and accountability but also fostering support and buy-in for their efficiency initiatives.

As they make plans to review feedback from stakeholders and adjust their communication strategies as needed, Alex feels a renewed sense of purpose and determination. With Sarah by his side and the support of their colleagues, he knows that they are well-equipped to achieve their goals. Together, they will continue to communicate progress to stakeholders, build trust and credibility, and propel the HR department towards even greater success.

8

Chapter 8: Overcoming Common Challenges

Addressing Resistance to Change

In the sleek, modern meeting room, Alex and Sarah reconvene their team to confront the challenging subpoint of addressing resistance to change. Surrounded by screens displaying strategies for change management and communication plans, they delve into the importance of understanding and mitigating resistance to ensure the success of their efficiency initiatives.

As they initiate the discussion, Alex feels a surge of determination. This is their opportunity to break down barriers and create a culture where change is embraced rather than feared.

But addressing resistance to change is no simple task. With entrenched habits and fear of the unknown to contend with, Alex finds himself grappling with uncertainty and doubt. How can they overcome resistance and rally their team behind their efforts to drive efficiency?

Yet Sarah remains steadfast, her experience in change management and organizational psychology a guiding light in the face of uncertainty. With her guidance, Alex learns to approach the challenge with empathy and patience, recognizing that change is a process that requires understanding and support.

Together, they develop a comprehensive plan for addressing resistance to change. They identify key stakeholders and engage them in the process, communicate the reasons for change and the benefits it will bring, and provide opportunities for feedback and input.

As they begin to implement their plan and address resistance to change, Alex feels a sense of optimism building within him. By fostering open communication and creating a supportive environment, they are not only overcoming resistance but also laying the foundation for a more agile and adaptable department.

As they make plans to monitor the progress of their change initiatives and adjust their strategies as needed, Alex feels a renewed sense of purpose and determination. With Sarah by his side and the support of their colleagues, he knows that they are well-equipped to overcome resistance to change and drive the HR department towards even greater success. Together, they will continue to navigate challenges, inspire change, and propel the department forward into a brighter future.

Dealing with Resource Constraints

In the sleek, modern meeting room, Alex and Sarah reconvene their team to confront the challenging subpoint of dealing with resource constraints. Surrounded by screens displaying budget spreadsheets and resource allocation plans, they delve into the

CHAPTER 8: OVERCOMING COMMON CHALLENGES

importance of creativity and resourcefulness in overcoming limitations and achieving their efficiency goals.

As they initiate the discussion, Alex feels a surge of determination. This is their opportunity to find innovative solutions and make the most of the resources they have, even in the face of constraints.

But dealing with resource constraints is no easy task. With limited budgets and competing priorities, Alex finds himself grappling with uncertainty and doubt. How can they accomplish their efficiency objectives with scarce resources at their disposal?

Yet Sarah remains steadfast, her experience in strategic planning and resource management a guiding light in the face of uncertainty. With her guidance, Alex learns to approach the challenge with flexibility and ingenuity, recognizing that constraints can often lead to creative solutions.

Together, they brainstorm ideas for maximizing their resources and optimizing their efficiency initiatives. They explore options such as reallocating funds from less critical areas, leveraging technology to automate tasks and streamline processes, and partnering with other departments or external vendors to share resources and expertise.

As they begin to implement their strategies and make the most of their resources, Alex feels a sense of empowerment building within him. By embracing resource constraints as an opportunity for innovation, they are not only overcoming limitations but also paving the way for greater efficiency and sustainability.

As they make plans to monitor their progress and adapt their strategies as needed, Alex feels a renewed sense of purpose and determination. With Sarah by his side and the support of their colleagues, he knows that they are well-equipped to tackle resource constraints and drive the HR department towards even greater success. Together, they will continue to find creative solutions, overcome challenges, and propel the department forward into a brighter future.

Managing Complexity in System Design

In the sleek, modern meeting room, Alex and Sarah gather their team to address the daunting subpoint of managing complexity in system design. Surrounded by screens displaying intricate system diagrams and project plans, they delve into the importance of simplicity and clarity in designing efficient and sustainable systems.

As they initiate the discussion, Alex feels a surge of determination. This is their opportunity to untangle the web of complexity and create streamlined systems that support their efficiency goals.

But managing complexity in system design is no small feat. With interconnected processes and interdependent components to consider, Alex finds himself grappling with uncertainty and doubt. How can they design systems that are both comprehensive and easy to understand?

Yet Sarah remains steadfast, her expertise in systems thinking and process optimization a beacon of guidance in the face of uncertainty. With her guidance, Alex learns to approach the challenge with a focus on simplicity and efficiency, recognizing that complexity often leads to inefficiency and confusion.

Together, they brainstorm ideas for simplifying their system design and streamlining their processes. They identify redundancies and bottlenecks, streamline workflows and eliminate unnecessary steps, and standardize procedures to create consistency and clarity.

As they begin to implement their strategies and redesign their systems, Alex feels a sense of clarity and purpose building within him. By managing complexity in system design, they are not only improving efficiency but also enhancing the overall effectiveness and sustainability of the department.

As they make plans to monitor the performance of their redesigned systems and make adjustments as needed, Alex feels a renewed sense of confidence and determination. With Sarah by his side and the support of their colleagues, he knows that they are well-equipped to tackle complexity and drive the HR department towards even greater success. Together, they will continue to simplify their systems, optimize their processes, and propel the department forward into a brighter future.

Handling Unforeseen Obstacles During Implementation

In the sleek, modern meeting room, Alex and Sarah reconvene their team to confront the challenging subpoint of handling unforeseen obstacles during implementation. Surrounded by screens displaying risk management plans and contingency strategies, they delve into the importance of resilience and adaptability in navigating unexpected challenges that may arise during the implementation of efficiency initiatives.

As they initiate the discussion, Alex feels a surge of determination. This is their chance to prepare for the unexpected, to develop strategies for overcoming obstacles and keeping their efficiency initiatives on track.

But handling unforeseen obstacles during implementation is no simple task. With numerous variables and uncertainties to consider, Alex finds himself grappling with uncertainty and doubt. How can they anticipate and mitigate risks to ensure the success of their implementation efforts?

Yet Sarah remains steadfast, her experience in project management and crisis response a guiding light in the face of uncertainty. With her guidance, Alex learns to approach the challenge with agility and foresight, recognizing that resilience is often the key to overcoming unexpected obstacles.

Together, they brainstorm potential risks and develop contingency plans to address them. They identify key stakeholders and establish communication channels to ensure that everyone is informed and prepared to respond to unforeseen challenges. They also build flexibility into their implementation timeline and budget to accommodate unexpected delays or setbacks.

As they begin to implement their contingency plans and navigate unforeseen obstacles, Alex feels a sense of determination building within him. By proactively addressing risks and building resilience into their implementation strategy, they are not only mitigating potential disruptions but also strengthening their ability to adapt and thrive in the face of adversity.

As they make plans to monitor their progress and adjust their strategies as needed, Alex feels a renewed sense of confidence and determination. With Sarah by his side and the support of their colleagues, he knows that they are well-equipped to handle whatever challenges may come their way. Together, they will continue to navigate obstacles, overcome setbacks, and propel the HR department towards even greater success.

CHAPTER 8: OVERCOMING COMMON CHALLENGES

Maintaining Momentum and Preventing Complacency

In the sleek, modern meeting room, Alex and Sarah reconvene their team to address the critical subpoint of maintaining momentum and preventing complacency. Surrounded by screens displaying motivational quotes and action plans, they delve into the importance of sustaining energy and enthusiasm to keep their efficiency initiatives on track.

As they initiate the discussion, Alex feels a surge of determination. This is their opportunity to keep the momentum going, to ensure that their efforts towards efficiency continue to drive progress and innovation.

But maintaining momentum and preventing complacency is no easy task. With the initial excitement of implementation fading and the day-to-day demands of work taking precedence, Alex finds himself grappling with uncertainty and doubt. How can they keep their team motivated and engaged for the long haul?

Yet Sarah remains steadfast, her experience in leadership development and employee engagement a guiding light in the face of uncertainty. With her guidance, Alex learns to approach the challenge with creativity and empathy, recognizing that sustaining momentum is as much about mindset as it is about action.

Together, they brainstorm strategies for maintaining momentum and preventing complacency. They celebrate small wins and milestones to keep morale high, provide ongoing training and development opportunities to keep skills sharp, and foster a culture of continuous improvement and innovation.

As they begin to implement their strategies and keep the momentum going, Alex feels a sense of purpose and determination building within him. By proactively addressing potential sources of complacency and keeping their team engaged and motivated, they are not only sustaining their efficiency initiatives but also laying the foundation for long-term success and growth.

As they make plans to monitor their progress and adjust their strategies as needed, Alex feels a renewed sense of confidence and determination. With Sarah by his side and the support of their colleagues, he knows that they are well-equipped to maintain momentum and drive the HR department towards even greater success. Together, they will continue to inspire their team, overcome challenges, and propel the department forward into a brighter future.

Learning from Setbacks and Adapting Strategies Accordingly

In the sleek, modern meeting room, Alex and Sarah gather their team to address the pivotal subpoint of learning from setbacks and adapting strategies accordingly. Surrounded by screens displaying analysis reports and strategy documents, they delve into the importance of resilience and flexibility in responding to challenges and setbacks that may arise during their efficiency initiatives.

As they initiate the discussion, Alex feels a surge of determination. This is their chance to turn setbacks into opportunities for growth and learning, to refine their strategies and emerge stronger from adversity.

But learning from setbacks and adapting strategies accordingly is no small feat. With the sting of failure fresh in their minds and uncertainty about the future, Alex finds himself grappling with doubt and apprehension. How can they pivot and adjust their approach to overcome obstacles and continue making progress towards their goals?

Yet Sarah remains steadfast, her experience in change management and organizational learning a beacon of guidance in the face of uncertainty. With her guidance, Alex learns to approach setbacks with curiosity and resilience, recognizing that failure is not the end but rather a stepping stone on the path to success.

Together, they reflect on past setbacks and analyze the factors that contributed to their challenges. They identify lessons learned and areas for improvement, and brainstorm new strategies and approaches to address them.

As they begin to implement their revised strategies and adapt their approach, Alex feels a sense of determination building within him. By learning from setbacks and embracing change, they are not only building resilience as a team but also positioning themselves for future success and growth.

As they make plans to monitor their progress and adjust their strategies as needed, Alex feels a renewed sense of purpose and determination. With Sarah by his side and the support of their colleagues, he knows that they are well-equipped to learn from setbacks, adapt their strategies, and propel the HR department towards even greater success. Together, they will continue to face challenges head-on, embrace change, and emerge stronger and more resilient than before.

Chapter 9: Scaling Efficiency for Growth

Planning for Scalability from the Outset

In the sleek, modern meeting room, Alex and Sarah reconvene their team to delve into the crucial subpoint of planning for scalability from the outset. Surrounded by screens displaying project timelines and scalability models, they emphasize the importance of laying a solid foundation to support the department's growth trajectory.

As they initiate the discussion, Alex feels a surge of determination. This is their chance to ensure that every decision and action they take is aligned with the long-term vision of scalability and sustainability.

But planning for scalability from the outset is no small feat. With competing priorities and the temptation to focus solely on immediate needs, Alex finds himself grappling with uncertainty and doubt. How can they balance the demands of the present with the needs of the future?

Yet Sarah remains steadfast, her experience in strategic planning and foresight a guiding light in the face of uncertainty. With her guidance, Alex learns to approach the challenge with clarity and intention, recognizing that scalability requires proactive planning and thoughtful consideration of potential challenges and opportunities.

Together, they develop a comprehensive plan for planning for scalability from the outset. They establish clear goals and objectives, conduct thorough market research and analysis to identify growth opportunities, and build flexibility into their strategies to accommodate future expansion.

As they begin to implement their plan and lay the groundwork for scalability, Alex feels a sense of purpose and determination building within him. By planning for scalability from the outset, they are not only setting themselves up for future success but also demonstrating their commitment to long-term growth and sustainability.

As they make plans to monitor their progress and adjust their strategies as needed, Alex feels a renewed sense of confidence and optimism. With Sarah by his side and the support of their colleagues, he knows that they are well-equipped to plan for scalability and drive the HR department towards even greater success. Together, they will continue to innovate, adapt, and pave the way for a future filled with endless possibilities.

Identifying Opportunities for Expansion

In the sleek, modern meeting room, Alex and Sarah reconvene their team to tackle the pivotal subpoint of identifying opportunities for expansion. Surrounded by screens displaying market research and growth projections, they emphasize the importance of strategic foresight and innovation in seizing opportunities for the department's growth.

As they initiate the discussion, Alex feels a surge of excitement. This is their chance to explore new horizons, to uncover potential avenues for expansion that will propel the department to new heights of success.

But identifying opportunities for expansion is no small task. With a vast landscape of possibilities and uncertainties to navigate, Alex finds himself grappling with uncertainty and doubt. How can they identify the right opportunities amidst the myriad of choices available?

Yet Sarah remains steadfast, her experience in market analysis and strategic planning a guiding light in the face of uncertainty. With her guidance, Alex learns to approach the challenge with curiosity and creativity, recognizing that opportunities for expansion often lie in unexpected places.

Together, they brainstorm ideas for potential areas of expansion and conduct thorough research to assess their viability. They analyze market trends and customer needs, identify gaps in the current offerings, and explore new technologies and innovations that could open doors to new opportunities.

As they begin to uncover promising opportunities for expansion, Alex feels a sense of anticipation building within him. By identifying opportunities for expansion, they are not only positioning themselves for future growth but also staying ahead of the curve in a rapidly evolving landscape.

As they make plans to explore further and develop strategies to capitalize on the identified opportunities, Alex feels a renewed sense of purpose and determination. With Sarah by his side and the support of their colleagues, he knows that they are well-equipped to identify and seize opportunities for expansion, driving the HR department towards even greater success. Together, they will continue to innovate, adapt, and pave the way for a future filled with endless possibilities.

Replicating Successful Systems in New Contexts

In the sleek, modern meeting room, Alex and Sarah convene their team to address the pivotal subpoint of replicating successful systems in new contexts. Surrounded by screens displaying case studies and best practices, they emphasize the importance of leveraging proven strategies and processes to drive expansion and efficiency across different contexts.

As they initiate the discussion, Alex feels a surge of determination. This is their opportunity to capitalize on their successes and leverage them to propel the department's growth into new territories.

But replicating successful systems in new contexts is no small feat. With diverse environments and unique challenges to consider, Alex finds himself grappling with uncertainty and doubt. How can they ensure that what works in one context will translate effectively to another?

Yet Sarah remains steadfast, her experience in cross-functional collaboration and process optimization a guiding light in the face of uncertainty. With her guidance, Alex learns to approach the challenge with adaptability and agility, recognizing that success often lies in the ability to tailor strategies to fit specific contexts.

Together, they analyze successful systems and processes that have yielded positive results in their current context. They identify key principles and components that can be replicated and adapted to new environments, ensuring that they maintain consistency and effectiveness while allowing for necessary adjustments.

As they begin to develop strategies for replicating successful systems in new contexts, Alex feels a sense of anticipation building within him. By leveraging proven strategies and processes, they are not only accelerating their expansion but also ensuring continuity and consistency in their approach.

As they make plans to implement their strategies and monitor their progress, Alex feels a renewed sense of purpose and determination. With Sarah by his side and the support of their colleagues, he knows that they are well-equipped to replicate successful systems in new contexts and drive the HR department towards even greater success. Together, they will continue to innovate, adapt, and pave the way for a future filled with endless possibilities.

Streamlining Processes to Accommodate Growth

In the sleek, modern meeting room, Alex and Sarah reconvene their team to delve into the critical subpoint of streamlining processes to accommodate growth. Surrounded by screens displaying flowcharts and efficiency metrics, they emphasize the importance of optimizing workflows to support the department's expansion plans.

As they initiate the discussion, Alex feels a surge of determination. This is their opportunity to ensure that their processes are scalable and efficient, capable of meeting the demands of a rapidly growing organization.

But streamlining processes to accommodate growth is no small task. With increased complexity and higher volumes of work to contend with, Alex finds himself grappling with uncertainty and doubt. How can they streamline their processes without sacrificing quality or effectiveness?

Yet Sarah remains steadfast, her experience in process optimization and automation a guiding light in the face of uncertainty. With her guidance, Alex learns to approach the challenge with systematic analysis and innovation, recognizing that streamlining processes is essential for long-term success.

Together, they review existing processes and identify areas for improvement. They eliminate bottlenecks, automate repetitive tasks, and standardize procedures to create consistency and efficiency across the department.

As they begin to implement their streamlined processes, Alex feels a sense of anticipation building within him. By streamlining processes to accommodate growth, they are not only increasing efficiency but also laying the foundation for sustainable expansion.

As they make plans to monitor their progress and refine their processes as needed, Alex feels a renewed sense of purpose and determination. With Sarah by his side and the support of their colleagues, he knows that they are well-equipped to streamline processes and drive the HR department towards even greater success. Together, they will continue to innovate, adapt, and pave the way for a future filled with endless possibilities.

Investing in Infrastructure and Technology Upgrades

In the sleek, modern meeting room, Alex and Sarah reconvene their team to tackle the crucial subpoint of investing in infrastructure and technology upgrades. Surrounded by screens displaying IT plans and equipment specifications, they emphasize the importance of staying ahead of the curve to support the department's growth and efficiency goals.

As they initiate the discussion, Alex feels a surge of determination. This is their opportunity to modernize their infrastructure and leverage cutting-edge technology to propel the department forward.

But investing in infrastructure and technology upgrades is no small feat. With budget constraints and competing priorities to consider, Alex finds himself grappling with uncertainty and doubt. How can they prioritize investments to maximize their impact and ensure long-term sustainability?

Yet Sarah remains steadfast, her expertise in technology implementation and project management a guiding light in the face of uncertainty. With her guidance, Alex learns to approach the challenge with strategic foresight and innovation, recognizing that investing in infrastructure and technology is essential for staying competitive in today's fast-paced environment.

Together, they assess their current infrastructure and technology systems and identify areas for improvement. They prioritize investments based on their potential to drive efficiency and support growth, whether it's upgrading hardware and software, implementing new systems and tools, or investing in training and development for their team.

As they begin to implement their technology upgrades and infrastructure improvements, Alex feels a sense of anticipation building within him. By investing in infrastructure and technology upgrades, they are not only modernizing their operations but also future-proofing the department for continued success.

As they make plans to monitor their progress and measure the impact of their investments, Alex feels a renewed sense of purpose and determination. With Sarah by his side and the support of their colleagues, he knows that they are well-equipped to invest in infrastructure and technology upgrades and drive the HR department towards even greater success. Together, they will continue to innovate, adapt, and pave the way for a future filled with endless possibilities.

Continuously Refining Systems to Meet Evolving Needs

In the sleek, modern meeting room, Alex and Sarah reconvene their team to tackle the pivotal subpoint of continuously refining systems to meet evolving needs. Surrounded by screens displaying feedback loops and iterative improvement plans, they emphasize the importance of agility and adaptability in responding to changing circumstances and demands.

As they initiate the discussion, Alex feels a surge of determination. This is their opportunity to foster a culture of innovation and continuous improvement, ensuring that their systems and processes remain aligned with the department's evolving needs.

But continuously refining systems to meet evolving needs is no small feat. With rapid changes in technology and market dynamics to contend with, Alex finds himself grappling with uncertainty and doubt. How can they stay ahead of the curve and anticipate future needs before they arise?

Yet Sarah remains steadfast, her experience in change management and organizational agility a guiding light in the face of uncertainty. With her guidance, Alex learns to approach the challenge with curiosity and flexibility, recognizing that the ability to adapt quickly is essential for long-term success.

Together, they establish feedback mechanisms and communication channels to gather insights and input from stakeholders. They conduct regular reviews and evaluations of their systems and processes, identifying areas for improvement and implementing changes in real-time.

As they begin to refine their systems and processes to meet evolving needs, Alex feels a sense of anticipation building within him. By embracing change and fostering a culture of continuous improvement, they are not only staying ahead of the curve but also positioning themselves as leaders in their industry.

As they make plans to monitor their progress and adjust their strategies as needed, Alex feels a renewed sense of purpose and determination. With Sarah by his side and the support of their colleagues, he knows that they are well-equipped to continuously refine systems and meet the HR department's evolving needs. Together, they will continue to innovate, adapt, and pave the way for a future filled with endless possibilities.

10

Chapter 10: Sustainability and Efficiency

Exploring the Relationship Between Efficiency and Sustainability

In the serene, eco-conscious meeting room, Alex and Sarah lead their team into a deep exploration of the relationship between efficiency and sustainability. Surrounded by screens displaying research articles and sustainability frameworks, they emphasize the interconnectedness of these two critical concepts.

As they initiate the discussion, Alex feels a sense of curiosity. This is their chance to uncover the synergies between efficiency and sustainability, and how their intertwining can lead to greater organizational success.

But exploring the relationship between efficiency and sustainability is no simple task. With complex systems and multifaceted challenges to consider, Alex finds himself grappling with uncertainty and doubt. How can they navigate this intricate relationship to drive positive change?

Yet Sarah remains steadfast, her expertise in sustainability practices and organizational efficiency a guiding light in the face of uncertainty. With her guidance, Alex learns to approach the challenge with open-mindedness and strategic thinking, recognizing that the alignment of efficiency and sustainability is essential for long-term prosperity.

Together, they delve into the intricacies of the relationship between efficiency and sustainability. They discuss how optimizing processes and minimizing waste can reduce environmental impact and enhance resource efficiency. They also explore how investing in sustainable practices, such as renewable energy and ethical sourcing, can lead to cost savings and competitive advantage.

As they uncover the interconnections between efficiency and sustainability, Alex feels a sense of enlightenment building within him. By embracing sustainability as a core principle of efficiency, they are not only driving organizational success but also contributing to a more sustainable future for generations to come.

As they make plans to integrate sustainability considerations into their efficiency initiatives and measure their impact on environmental and social outcomes, Alex feels a renewed sense of purpose and determination. With Sarah by his side and the support of their colleagues, he knows that they are well-equipped to lead the HR department towards a future where efficiency and sustainability are intertwined. Together, they will continue to innovate, adapt, and pave the way for a future filled with endless possibilities.

Reducing Environmental Impact Through Efficient Practices

In the serene, eco-conscious meeting room, Alex and Sarah guide their team through an exploration of how efficient practices can significantly reduce environmental impact. Surrounded by screens displaying sustainability reports and efficiency case studies, they emphasize the power of small changes in driving positive environmental outcomes.

As they initiate the discussion, Alex feels a sense of urgency. This is their opportunity to uncover practical ways to minimize their ecological footprint and contribute to a healthier planet.

But reducing environmental impact through efficient practices is no easy feat. With entrenched habits and systemic challenges to overcome, Alex finds himself grappling with uncertainty and doubt. How can they implement changes that not only benefit the environment but also maintain productivity and profitability?

Yet Sarah remains steadfast, her commitment to environmental stewardship and efficiency a guiding light in the face of uncertainty. With her guidance, Alex learns to approach the challenge with creativity and determination, recognizing that even small changes can have a significant impact when multiplied across an organization.

Together, they brainstorm strategies for reducing environmental impact through efficient practices. They discuss initiatives such as minimizing paper usage, optimizing energy consumption, and promoting eco-friendly commuting options.

As they delve deeper into the discussion, Alex feels a sense of empowerment building within him. By embracing efficient practices, they are not only reducing costs and improving efficiency but also making a tangible difference in the health of the planet.

As they make plans to implement their initiatives and monitor their progress towards reducing environmental impact, Alex feels a renewed sense of purpose and determination. With Sarah by his side and the support of their colleagues, he knows that they are well-equipped to lead the HR department towards a future where sustainability is a core principle of efficiency. Together, they will continue to innovate, adapt, and pave the way for a future filled with endless possibilities, all while leaving a positive impact on the environment.

Incorporating Sustainability into System Design

In the serene, eco-conscious meeting room, Alex and Sarah guide their team through a critical exploration of incorporating sustainability into system design. Surrounded by screens displaying blueprints and sustainability frameworks, they emphasize the importance of integrating environmental considerations into every aspect of their operations.

As they initiate the discussion, Alex feels a sense of purpose. This is their chance to redesign their systems and processes with sustainability at the forefront, ensuring that every decision they make contributes to a greener, more sustainable future.

But incorporating sustainability into system design is no simple task. With entrenched practices and traditional mindsets to overcome, Alex finds himself grappling with uncertainty and doubt. How can they shift their approach to prioritize sustainability without sacrificing efficiency or effectiveness?

Yet Sarah remains steadfast, her passion for environmental stewardship and innovation a guiding light in the face of uncertainty. With her guidance, Alex learns to approach the challenge with vision and determination, recognizing that sustainability is not a burden but an opportunity for innovation and progress.

Together, they brainstorm ways to incorporate sustainability into system design. They discuss initiatives such as designing products and services with minimal environmental impact, optimizing supply chains to reduce carbon emissions, and implementing circular economy principles to minimize waste.

As they delve deeper into the discussion, Alex feels a sense of inspiration building within him. By integrating sustainability into system design, they are not only future-proofing their operations but also leading the way towards a more sustainable future for all.

As they make plans to implement their initiatives and monitor their progress towards incorporating sustainability into system design, Alex feels a renewed sense of purpose and determination. With Sarah by his side and the support of their colleagues, he knows that they are well-equipped to lead the HR department towards a future where sustainability is not just a goal, but a fundamental principle guiding every decision they make. Together, they will continue to innovate, adapt, and pave the way for a future filled with endless possibilities, all while leaving a positive impact on the environment.

Engaging with Stakeholders on Sustainability Initiatives

In the serene, eco-conscious meeting room, Alex and Sarah lead their team through a crucial exploration of engaging with stakeholders on sustainability initiatives. Surrounded by screens displaying stakeholder engagement plans and sustainability communication strategies, they emphasize the importance of building partnerships and fostering dialogue to drive meaningful change.

As they initiate the discussion, Alex feels a sense of purpose. This is their opportunity to rally support and mobilize their stakeholders towards a shared vision of sustainability and efficiency.

But engaging with stakeholders on sustainability initiatives is no small feat. With diverse perspectives and interests to consider, Alex finds himself grappling with uncertainty and doubt. How can they navigate the complexities of stakeholder engagement to ensure that everyone is aligned and committed to their sustainability goals?

Yet Sarah remains steadfast, her expertise in stakeholder management and communication a guiding light in the face of uncertainty. With her guidance, Alex learns to approach the challenge with empathy and transparency, recognizing that meaningful engagement is key to driving lasting change.

Together, they develop a comprehensive stakeholder engagement strategy. They identify key stakeholders, including employees, customers, suppliers, and community members, and tailor their communication approach to resonate with each group.

As they begin to engage with stakeholders on sustainability initiatives, Alex feels a sense of empowerment building within him. By fostering dialogue and building partnerships, they are not only amplifying the impact of their sustainability efforts but also creating a sense of shared ownership and responsibility.

As they make plans to implement their engagement strategy and monitor their progress towards building a coalition of support for their sustainability initiatives, Alex feels a renewed sense of purpose and determination. With Sarah by his side and the support of their colleagues, he knows that they are well-equipped to lead the HR department towards a future where sustainability is not just a goal, but a shared commitment embraced by all. Together, they will continue to innovate, adapt, and pave the way for a future filled with endless possibilities, all while leaving a positive impact on the environment and society.

Measuring and Reporting on Sustainability Efforts

In the serene, eco-conscious meeting room, Alex and Sarah guide their team through the critical subpoint of measuring and reporting on sustainability efforts. Surrounded by screens displaying sustainability metrics and reporting frameworks, they emphasize the importance of accountability and transparency in tracking progress towards their sustainability goals.

As they initiate the discussion, Alex feels a sense of determination. This is their opportunity to demonstrate the tangible impact of their sustainability initiatives and hold themselves accountable to their stakeholders.

But measuring and reporting on sustainability efforts is no small task. With complex data and diverse stakeholders to consider, Alex finds himself grappling with uncertainty and doubt. How can they effectively capture and communicate the progress they've made towards their sustainability goals?

Yet Sarah remains steadfast, her expertise in sustainability reporting and communication a guiding light in the face of uncertainty. With her guidance, Alex learns to approach the challenge with rigor and clarity, recognizing that transparent reporting is essential for building trust and credibility.

Together, they develop a robust measurement and reporting framework. They identify key performance indicators (KPIs) to track their progress towards sustainability targets, such as carbon emissions reductions, waste diversion rates, and energy efficiency improvements.

As they begin to measure their sustainability efforts and compile their findings into a comprehensive report, Alex feels a sense of pride building within him. By transparently reporting on their sustainability initiatives, they are not only holding themselves accountable but also inspiring others to take action and join their journey towards a more sustainable future.

As they make plans to share their sustainability report with stakeholders and communicate their progress towards their sustainability goals, Alex feels a renewed sense of purpose and determination. With Sarah by his side and the support of their colleagues, he knows that they are well-equipped to lead the HR department towards a future where sustainability is not just a goal, but a fundamental principle guiding every decision they make. Together, they will continue to innovate, adapt, and pave the way for a future filled with endless possibilities, all while leaving a positive impact on the environment and society.

Integrating Sustainability Goals into the Overall Efficiency Blueprint

In the serene, eco-conscious meeting room, Alex and Sarah lead their team through a pivotal discussion on integrating sustainability goals into the overall efficiency blueprint. Surrounded by screens displaying interconnected diagrams of efficiency and sustainability initiatives, they emphasize the importance of weaving environmental stewardship into the fabric of every operational decision.

As they initiate the discussion, Alex feels a sense of urgency. This is their opportunity to create a blueprint for success that not only optimizes efficiency but also champions sustainability at every turn.

But integrating sustainability goals into the overall efficiency blueprint is no small feat. With competing priorities and complex systems to navigate, Alex finds himself grappling with uncertainty and doubt. How can they strike the right balance between efficiency gains and environmental responsibility?

Yet Sarah remains steadfast, her vision for a harmonious blend of efficiency and sustainability guiding the way forward. With her guidance, Alex learns to approach the challenge with holistic thinking and strategic foresight, recognizing that true success lies in aligning their efficiency efforts with their broader sustainability objectives.

Together, they analyze each component of the efficiency blueprint, identifying opportunities to infuse sustainability goals into every aspect of their operations. They explore ways to minimize resource consumption, reduce waste, and promote eco-friendly practices throughout the organization.

As they delve deeper into the discussion, Alex feels a sense of purpose building within him. By integrating sustainability goals into the overall efficiency blueprint, they are not only driving performance and profitability but also paving the way for a more sustainable future.

As they make plans to implement their integrated efficiency and sustainability blueprint and monitor their progress towards their shared goals, Alex feels a renewed sense of determination. With Sarah by his side and the support of their colleagues, he knows that they are well-equipped to lead the HR department towards a future where efficiency and sustainability are deeply intertwined. Together, they will continue to innovate, adapt, and pave the way for a future filled with endless possibilities, all while leaving a positive impact on the environment and society.

11

Chapter 11: Case Studies in Efficiency

Examining Real-World Examples of Efficiency Improvement

In the sleek, modern meeting room, Alex and Sarah lead their team through a deep dive into real-world examples of efficiency improvement, drawing inspiration from organizations that have paved the way in optimizing their operations. Surrounded by screens displaying case studies and success stories, they emphasize the importance of learning from the experiences of companies like Google, Toyota, and Unilever.

As they initiate the discussion, Alex feels a sense of anticipation. This is their opportunity to glean insights from industry leaders and apply them to their own efficiency journey.

But examining real-world examples of efficiency improvement is no small feat. With a myriad of success stories and best practices to consider, Alex finds himself grappling with the challenge of distilling the most relevant lessons for their own organization.

Yet Sarah remains steadfast, her expertise in analysis and synthesis shining through as she guides the team through the complexities of each case study. With her guidance, Alex learns to approach the challenge with discernment, recognizing that while each organization's journey is unique, there are valuable insights to be gained from studying their strategies and approaches.

Together, they delve into the efficiency initiatives of companies like Google, renowned for its data-driven approach to process optimization, Toyota, celebrated for its pioneering work in lean manufacturing, and Unilever, recognized for its commitment to sustainability and supply chain efficiency.

As they analyze each case study in detail, Alex feels a sense of inspiration building within him. By examining real-world examples of efficiency improvement, they are not only expanding their knowledge but also gaining practical insights that can inform their own strategies and initiatives.

As they make plans to distill the key learnings from the case studies and apply them to their own operations, Alex feels a renewed sense of purpose and determination. With Sarah by his side and the support of their colleagues, he knows that they are well-equipped to lead the HR department towards a future defined by efficiency, innovation, and sustainable success. Together, they will continue to innovate, adapt, and pave the way for a future filled with endless possibilities, drawing inspiration from the successes of industry leaders.

Highlighting Successful Implementation Strategies

In the sleek, modern meeting room, Alex and Sarah guide their team through an exploration of successful implementation strategies gleaned from real-world examples of efficiency improvement. Surrounded by screens displaying case studies and implementation frameworks, they emphasize the importance of strategic execution in translating ideas into tangible results.

As they initiate the discussion, Alex feels a sense of excitement. This is their chance to uncover the key strategies and tactics that have enabled organizations to successfully implement efficiency initiatives and drive sustainable change.

But highlighting successful implementation strategies is no small task. With a multitude of factors and variables at play, Alex finds himself grappling with the challenge of distilling the most impactful strategies for their own organization.

Yet Sarah remains steadfast, her expertise in project management and change implementation shining through as she guides the team through the complexities of each case study. With her guidance, Alex learns to approach the challenge with a strategic mindset, recognizing that successful implementation requires careful planning, clear communication, and unwavering commitment.

Together, they delve into the implementation strategies of companies like Amazon, known for its relentless focus on customer satisfaction and continuous improvement, IKEA, celebrated for its innovative approach to supply chain optimization, and Starbucks, recognized for its employee-centric culture and emphasis on operational efficiency.

As they analyze each case study in detail, Alex feels a sense of inspiration building within him. By highlighting successful implementation strategies, they are not only gaining valuable insights but also identifying actionable steps that can drive meaningful change within their own organization.

As they make plans to incorporate these strategies into their own efficiency initiatives and develop a roadmap for implementation, Alex feels a renewed sense of purpose and determination. With Sarah by his side and the support of their colleagues, he knows that they are well-equipped to lead the HR department towards a future defined by efficiency, innovation, and sustainable success. Together, they will continue to innovate, adapt, and pave the way for a future filled with endless possibilities, drawing inspiration from the successful implementation strategies of industry leaders.

Learning from Challenges and Setbacks

In the sleek, modern meeting room, Alex and Sarah lead their team through an introspective exploration of learning from challenges and setbacks in the pursuit of efficiency. Surrounded by screens displaying case studies and post-mortem analyses, they emphasize the importance of resilience and adaptability in the face of adversity.

As they initiate the discussion, Alex feels a sense of humility. This is their opportunity to acknowledge the inevitability of challenges and setbacks, and to extract valuable lessons from their experiences.

But learning from challenges and setbacks is no easy task. With the sting of past failures still fresh in their minds, Alex finds himself grappling with the discomfort of revisiting past mistakes.

Yet Sarah remains steadfast, her wisdom and empathy serving as a beacon of guidance for the team. With her encouragement, Alex learns to approach the challenge with openness and vulnerability, recognizing that true growth often arises from moments of struggle.

Together, they delve into the challenges and setbacks faced by organizations like Apple, confronted with supply chain disruptions and product recalls, and Tesla, navigating production delays and quality control issues.

As they analyze each case study with a critical eye, Alex feels a sense of empathy building within him. By learning from the challenges and setbacks of others, they are not only gaining valuable insights but also cultivating a culture of continuous improvement and resilience within their own team.

As they make plans to incorporate these lessons into their own efficiency initiatives and develop strategies for mitigating future challenges, Alex feels a renewed sense of determination. With Sarah by his side and the support of their colleagues, he knows that they are well-equipped to lead the HR department towards a future defined by efficiency, innovation, and sustainable success. Together, they will continue to innovate, adapt, and pave the way for a future filled with endless possibilities, drawing strength from the lessons learned from challenges and setbacks.

Drawing Lessons and Insights from Case Studies

In the sleek, modern meeting room, Alex and Sarah guide their team through a profound examination of drawing lessons and insights from case studies in efficiency. Surrounded by screens displaying detailed analyses and impactful anecdotes, they emphasize the transformative power of extracting wisdom from the experiences of others.

As they initiate the discussion, Alex feels a sense of anticipation. This is their chance to distill the most valuable lessons and insights from a diverse array of case studies, shaping their own efficiency journey with newfound knowledge and clarity.

But drawing lessons and insights from case studies is no small feat. With a multitude of examples and perspectives to consider, Alex finds himself grappling with the challenge of identifying the most relevant takeaways for their own organization.

Yet Sarah remains steadfast, her analytical prowess and strategic thinking guiding the team through the intricacies of each case study. With her guidance, Alex learns to approach the challenge with focus and discernment, recognizing that every case study offers unique insights that can inform their decision-making and drive meaningful change.

Together, they delve into the case studies with a spirit of curiosity and inquiry. They explore the successes and failures of organizations like Microsoft, hailed for its innovative approach to digital transformation, and Walmart, renowned for its unparalleled supply chain efficiency.

As they analyze each case study with rigor and depth, Alex feels a sense of enlightenment building within him. By drawing lessons and insights from case studies, they are not only expanding their knowledge but also gaining invaluable perspectives that can shape their own efficiency initiatives.

As they make plans to integrate these lessons into their own strategy and apply them to their organizational context, Alex feels a renewed sense of purpose and determination. With Sarah by his side and the support of their colleagues, he knows that they are well-equipped to lead the HR department towards a future defined by efficiency, innovation, and sustainable success. Together, they will continue to innovate, adapt, and pave the way for a future filled with endless possibilities, drawing inspiration from the lessons learned from case studies in efficiency.

Applying Principles to Readers' Own Contexts

In the sleek, modern meeting room, Alex and Sarah lead their team through a pivotal discussion on applying principles gleaned from case studies to their own contexts. Surrounded by screens displaying frameworks and implementation strategies, they emphasize the importance of translating theory into action and tailoring solutions to meet the unique needs of their organization.

As they initiate the discussion, Alex feels a sense of urgency. This is their opportunity to bridge the gap between theory and practice, equipping themselves with the tools and insights needed to drive meaningful change within their own organization.

But applying principles to their own contexts is no small feat. With a myriad of variables and considerations to account for, Alex finds himself grappling with the challenge of translating abstract concepts into tangible strategies.

Yet Sarah remains steadfast, her practical wisdom and strategic acumen serving as a guiding light for the team. With her guidance, Alex learns to approach the challenge with creativity and adaptability, recognizing that true innovation often arises from the intersection of theory and practice.

Together, they delve into the principles and best practices gleaned from case studies, identifying key insights and strategies that can be applied to their own organization. They discuss how to adapt and customize these principles to fit their unique context, taking into account factors such as organizational culture, resources, and goals.

As they brainstorm ideas and develop action plans, Alex feels a sense of empowerment building within him. By applying principles to their own contexts, they are not only gaining practical solutions but also laying the foundation for sustainable growth and success.

As they make plans to implement their strategies and monitor their progress, Alex feels a renewed sense of purpose and determination. With Sarah by his side and the support of their colleagues, he knows that they are well-equipped to lead the HR department towards a future defined by efficiency, innovation, and sustainable success. Together, they will continue to innovate, adapt, and pave the way for a future filled with endless possibilities, drawing inspiration from the principles gleaned from case studies in efficiency.

Inspiring Readers with Stories of Transformation

In the serene, modern meeting room, Alex and Sarah embark on a captivating journey of inspiring their team with stories of transformation. Surrounded by screens displaying narratives of resilience and innovation, they emphasize the power of storytelling in sparking motivation and driving change.

As they initiate the discussion, Alex feels a surge of anticipation. This is their chance to ignite a fire within their team, illuminating the path to transformation through the power of storytelling.

But inspiring readers with stories of transformation is no small feat. With the weight of expectations and the need to captivate hearts and minds, Alex finds himself grappling with the challenge of selecting the most compelling stories to share.

Yet Sarah remains steadfast, her storytelling prowess and empathy serving as a beacon of inspiration for the team. With her guidance, Alex learns to approach the challenge with authenticity and vulnerability, recognizing that true transformation often begins with a story.

Together, they weave tales of organizations that have overcome adversity and embraced change, such as Airbnb, born from a simple idea and transformed into a global phenomenon, and Patagonia, committed to sustainability and social responsibility from its inception.

As they delve into each story with passion and conviction, Alex feels a sense of connection building within him. By sharing stories of transformation, they are not only inspiring their team but also fostering a sense of camaraderie and shared purpose.

As they reflect on the lessons learned and the possibilities that lie ahead, Alex feels a renewed sense of hope and determination. With Sarah by his side and the support of their colleagues, he knows that they are well-equipped to lead the HR department towards a future defined by possibility, innovation, and sustainable success. Together, they will continue to innovate, adapt, and pave the way for a future filled with endless possibilities, drawing inspiration from the stories of transformation that have shaped their journey.

12

Chapter 12: Future Trends in Efficiency

Predicting Emerging Technologies and Trends

In the state-of-the-art meeting room, Alex and Sarah guide their team through a thought-provoking exploration of predicting emerging technologies and trends in efficiency. Surrounded by screens displaying futuristic concepts and cutting-edge innovations, they embark on a journey to anticipate the transformative forces that will shape the future of work.

As they initiate the discussion, Alex feels a surge of anticipation. This is their chance to peer into the crystal ball of technological advancement, to discern the trends that will revolutionize the way they work and live.

But predicting emerging technologies and trends is no easy feat. With the dizzying pace of technological change and the uncertainty of the future, Alex finds himself grappling with the challenge of separating hype from reality.

Yet Sarah remains steadfast, her foresight and analytical prowess guiding the team through the complexities of prediction. With her guidance, Alex learns to approach the challenge with a blend of skepticism and imagination, recognizing that while not all predictions will come to pass, it is essential to stay ahead of the curve.

Together, they explore a plethora of emerging technologies and trends, from the proliferation of artificial intelligence and robotics to the potential of blockchain and decentralized finance. They discuss the impact of quantum computing on data processing and the rise of biotechnology in shaping sustainable practices.

As they delve deeper into the discussion, Alex feels a sense of excitement building within him. By predicting emerging technologies and trends, they are not only preparing themselves for the future but also positioning their organization to seize new opportunities and drive innovation.

As they brainstorm ideas and develop strategies to harness these emerging technologies, Alex feels a renewed sense of purpose and determination. With Sarah by his side and the support of their colleagues, he knows that they are well-equipped to lead the HR department towards a future defined by technological advancement, creativity, and sustainable success. Together, they will continue to innovate, adapt, and pave the way for a future filled with endless possibilities, drawing inspiration from the emerging technologies and trends that hold the promise of a brighter tomorrow.

Anticipating Changes in Business Practices and Models

In the forward-thinking meeting room, Alex and Sarah lead their team through a dynamic exploration of anticipating changes in business practices and models. Surrounded by screens displaying market analyses and industry forecasts, they embark on a journey to anticipate the shifting landscape of business in the years to come.

As they initiate the discussion, Alex feels a surge of anticipation. This is their opportunity to peer into the future of commerce, to discern the evolving practices and models that will define success in the years ahead.

But anticipating changes in business practices and models is no simple task. With the dynamic nature of markets and the unpredictability of consumer behavior, Alex finds himself grappling with the challenge of navigating uncertainty and disruption.

Yet Sarah remains steadfast, her strategic acumen and market insights guiding the team through the complexities of anticipation. With her guidance, Alex learns to approach the challenge with agility and adaptability, recognizing that the ability to pivot and innovate will be critical in the face of change.

Together, they explore a multitude of potential changes in business practices and models, from the rise of platform-based ecosystems and the gig economy to the growing emphasis on sustainability and social responsibility. They discuss the impact of digitalization and automation on traditional business models and the shift towards agile and decentralized organizational structures.

As they delve deeper into the discussion, Alex feels a sense of excitement building within him. By anticipating changes in business practices and models, they are not only preparing themselves for the future but also positioning their organization to thrive in a rapidly evolving landscape.

As they brainstorm ideas and develop strategies to embrace these changes, Alex feels a renewed sense of purpose and determination. With Sarah by his side and the support of their colleagues, he knows that they are well-equipped to lead the HR department towards a future defined by innovation, resilience, and sustainable success. Together, they will continue to innovate, adapt, and pave the way for a future filled with endless possibilities, drawing inspiration from the changing business practices and models that lie ahead.

Considering the Impact of Globalization and Digitalization

In the visionary meeting room, Alex and Sarah delve into a profound exploration of considering the impact of globalization and digitalization on the future of efficiency. Surrounded by screens displaying global economic trends and digital transformation strategies, they embark on a journey to understand how these forces will shape the landscape of business and work.

As they initiate the discussion, Alex feels a sense of awe. This is their opportunity to dissect the seismic shifts brought about by globalization and digitalization, and to chart a course towards harnessing their transformative power.

But considering the impact of globalization and digitalization is no small feat. With the world becoming increasingly interconnected and technology evolving at breakneck speed, Alex finds himself grappling with the enormity of the task.

Yet Sarah remains steadfast, her deep understanding of global markets and digital trends serving as a beacon of guidance for the team. With her expertise, Alex learns to approach the challenge with clarity and insight, recognizing that while globalization and digitalization present challenges, they also offer unparalleled opportunities for innovation and growth.

Together, they explore the far-reaching impact of globalization and digitalization on business practices, supply chains, and consumer behavior. They discuss the rise of remote work and virtual collaboration, the emergence of new marketplaces and business models, and the importance of digital literacy and cybersecurity in the modern workplace.

As they delve deeper into the discussion, Alex feels a sense of clarity building within him. By considering the impact of globalization and digitalization, they are not only preparing themselves for the future but also positioning their organization to thrive in an increasingly interconnected and digital world.

As they brainstorm ideas and develop strategies to adapt to these changes, Alex feels a renewed sense of purpose and determination. With Sarah by his side and the support of their colleagues, he knows that they are well-equipped to lead the HR department towards a future defined by innovation, resilience, and sustainable success. Together, they will continue to innovate, adapt, and pave the way for a future filled with endless possibilities, drawing inspiration from the transformative forces of globalization and digitalization.

Exploring the Role of Artificial Intelligence and Machine Learning

In the technologically charged meeting room, Alex and Sarah delve into an illuminating exploration of the role of artificial intelligence and machine learning in shaping the future of efficiency. Surrounded by screens displaying algorithms and neural networks, they embark on a journey to understand how these cutting-edge technologies will revolutionize the way we work and live.

As they initiate the discussion, Alex feels a sense of wonder. This is their chance to unravel the mysteries of artificial intelligence and machine learning, and to unlock the potential of these transformative technologies.

But exploring the role of artificial intelligence and machine learning is no simple task. With the complexity of algorithms and the ethical implications of automation, Alex finds himself grappling with the enormity of the subject.

Yet Sarah remains steadfast, her expertise in data science and predictive analytics guiding the team through the intricacies of artificial intelligence and machine learning. With her guidance, Alex learns to approach the challenge with curiosity and discernment, recognizing that while these technologies hold immense promise, they also raise important questions about privacy, bias, and human dignity.

Together, they delve into the myriad applications of artificial intelligence and machine learning, from predictive analytics and natural language processing to autonomous systems and robotic process automation. They discuss the potential impact of these technologies on workforce dynamics, job roles, and organizational efficiency.

As they delve deeper into the discussion, Alex feels a sense of awe building within him. By exploring the role of artificial intelligence and machine learning, they are not only preparing themselves for the future but also unlocking new possibilities for innovation and growth.

As they brainstorm ideas and develop strategies to harness the power of these technologies, Alex feels a renewed sense of purpose and determination. With Sarah by his side and the support of their colleagues, he knows that they are well-equipped to lead the HR department towards a future defined by technological advancement, creativity, and sustainable success. Together, they will continue to innovate, adapt, and pave the way for a future filled with endless possibilities, drawing inspiration from the transformative potential of artificial intelligence and machine learning.

Discussing Ethical Implications of Efficiency-Driven Technologies

In the contemplative meeting room, Alex and Sarah lead their team through a thought-provoking discussion on the ethical implications of efficiency-driven technologies. Surrounded by screens displaying data privacy regulations and ethical frameworks, they embark on a journey to navigate the delicate balance between progress and responsibility in the digital age.

As they initiate the discussion, Alex feels a sense of gravity. This is their opportunity to confront the ethical dilemmas inherent in the pursuit of efficiency, and to ensure that their technological advancements are guided by principles of fairness, transparency, and respect for human dignity.

But discussing the ethical implications of efficiency-driven

CHAPTER 12: FUTURE TRENDS IN EFFICIENCY

technologies is no simple task. With the potential for unintended consequences and the need to safeguard against exploitation and discrimination, Alex finds himself grappling with the weight of responsibility.

Yet Sarah remains steadfast, her moral compass and empathy serving as a beacon of guidance for the team. With her leadership, Alex learns to approach the challenge with humility and integrity, recognizing that while efficiency is important, it must never come at the expense of ethical considerations.

Together, they delve into the ethical implications of technologies such as artificial intelligence, machine learning, and automation. They discuss concerns related to data privacy, algorithmic bias, and the impact of technology on job displacement and inequality.

As they navigate the complexities of the discussion, Alex feels a sense of urgency building within him. By discussing the ethical implications of efficiency-driven technologies, they are not only safeguarding against potential harms but also fostering a culture of responsible innovation and accountability.

As they brainstorm ideas and develop strategies to mitigate risks and uphold ethical standards, Alex feels a renewed sense of purpose and determination. With Sarah by his side and the support of their colleagues, he knows that they are well-equipped to lead the HR department towards a future defined by integrity, compassion, and sustainable success. Together, they will continue to innovate, adapt, and pave the way for a future filled with endless possibilities, drawing inspiration from their commitment to ethical excellence in the digital age.

Preparing for the Future of Work and Organizational Dynamics

The team finds themselves in the ultra-modern conference room of their newly opened innovation center. The room is filled with cutting-edge technology: smartboards, virtual reality headsets, and an AI-powered assistant ready to help. The topic of today's meeting is crucial—preparing for the future of work and organizational dynamics.

Alex, always the visionary, starts the discussion. "We've talked about emerging technologies, AI, and globalization. Now, let's focus on how these trends will reshape our work environment and organizational structure."

Sarah, the project manager, nods. "We need to be proactive in understanding how the future of work will evolve. This includes remote work, flexible schedules, and new collaboration tools. Our goal is to create a resilient organization that thrives in this new landscape."

Grace, the HR specialist, chimes in. "One of the biggest shifts we're seeing is the move towards remote and hybrid work models. We need to ensure our systems and processes support this flexibility while maintaining productivity and team cohesion."

Marcus, the tech enthusiast, gestures to the smartboard, which displays a graph of projected workforce trends. "We should leverage technology to facilitate this transition. Tools like virtual collaboration platforms, project management software, and AI-driven analytics will be crucial."

Alex adds, "It's not just about tools; it's about culture. We need to foster a culture of adaptability and continuous learning. Employees should feel empowered to embrace new technolo-

CHAPTER 12: FUTURE TRENDS IN EFFICIENCY

gies and work styles."

Priya, the quality control expert, speaks up. "Training and development will be key. We need to offer ongoing learning opportunities to ensure our team stays ahead of the curve. This includes upskilling in new technologies and developing soft skills for remote collaboration."

Daniel, the senior analyst, raises an important point. "We also need to consider organizational dynamics. Hierarchical structures might give way to more fluid, project-based teams. This will require a shift in how we manage and evaluate performance."

As the discussion progresses, the team brainstorms practical steps to prepare for these changes. They decide to pilot a flexible work program, allowing employees to choose remote or hybrid schedules. Marcus suggests implementing an AI-driven project management tool to streamline workflows and enhance virtual collaboration.

Grace proposes regular virtual town halls to keep everyone connected and aligned with the company's vision. "Communication is vital," she says. "We need to ensure everyone feels included and informed, regardless of where they work."

Sarah outlines a training program focused on digital literacy and remote work best practices. "We'll provide resources and workshops to help our team navigate this new environment effectively."

The meeting extends into the evening, filled with lively discussions and innovative ideas. By the end, they have a clear action plan. They will invest in technology, foster a culture of adaptability, and provide continuous learning opportunities to prepare for the future of work.

Alex looks around the room, his eyes reflecting both excitement and determination. "We're not just preparing for the future; we're shaping it. By embracing these changes, we'll build an organization that's resilient, dynamic, and ready to thrive in any environment."

In the following weeks, the team implements their plan with enthusiasm. They roll out the flexible work program, introduce new collaboration tools, and launch the training initiatives. The response from the employees is overwhelmingly positive, with many expressing appreciation for the company's forward-thinking approach.

As they navigate this transition, the team remains committed to continuous improvement. They regularly gather feedback, make adjustments, and celebrate their successes. The organization begins to evolve, becoming more agile, innovative, and prepared for the future.

The final scene in the innovation center encapsulates their journey. The team, joined by employees from various departments, stands around the conference room, looking at a digital display of their achievements and future goals. There's a sense of unity and shared purpose.

Sarah raises a toast. "To the future—one that we're not just ready for, but one we're excited to create. Together."

The room erupts in cheers, the sound echoing through the innovation center. They've laid the groundwork for sustainable success, and with their eyes firmly on the future, they're ready to take on whatever comes next.

13

Chapter 13: Continuous Improvement

Embracing a Culture of Innovation

In the vibrant meeting room, Alex and Sarah lead their team through an exhilarating exploration of embracing a culture of innovation. Surrounded by screens displaying brainstorming sessions and design thinking workshops, they embark on a journey to cultivate a workplace where creativity flourishes, and new ideas are celebrated.

As they initiate the discussion, Alex feels a surge of energy. This is their chance to unleash the full potential of their team, to inspire them to think boldly, and to create solutions that push the boundaries of what's possible.

But embracing a culture of innovation is not just about generating ideas—it's about creating an environment where experimentation is encouraged, failure is seen as a stepping stone to success, and every voice is valued.

Yet Sarah remains steadfast, her passion for innovation and her belief in the power of collaboration guiding the team through the intricacies of fostering creativity. With her leadership, Alex learns to approach the challenge with openness and curiosity, recognizing that innovation is not a solo endeavor but a collective effort fueled by diversity of thought and experience.

Together, they explore the essential elements of a culture of innovation, from fostering a sense of psychological safety to providing resources and support for experimentation. They discuss the importance of cross-functional collaboration, learning from failure, and celebrating successes, no matter how small.

As they delve deeper into the discussion, Alex feels a sense of excitement building within him. By embracing a culture of innovation, they are not only unlocking the creative potential of their team but also fostering a sense of ownership and empowerment that will drive meaningful change and growth.

As they brainstorm ideas and develop strategies to embed innovation into their organizational DNA, Alex feels a renewed sense of purpose and determination. With Sarah by his side and the support of their colleagues, he knows that they are well-equipped to lead the HR department towards a future defined by creativity, resilience, and sustainable success. Together, they will continue to innovate, adapt, and pave the way for a future filled with endless possibilities, drawing inspiration from the transformative power of a culture of innovation.

Integrating Feedback Loops for Continuous Improvement

In the interactive meeting room, Alex and Sarah guide their team through an insightful exploration of integrating feedback loops for continuous improvement. Surrounded by screens displaying feedback mechanisms and performance metrics, they embark on a journey to establish a system where learning and growth are woven into the fabric of their organization.

As they initiate the discussion, Alex feels a sense of anticipation. This is their opportunity to create a culture where feedback is not just welcomed but actively sought after, where every interaction becomes an opportunity for reflection and refinement.

But integrating feedback loops for continuous improvement is not just about collecting data—it's about creating a culture where feedback is valued, acted upon, and used to drive meaningful change.

Yet Sarah remains steadfast, her commitment to excellence and her belief in the power of feedback guiding the team through the complexities of implementation. With her guidance, Alex learns to approach the challenge with humility and openness, recognizing that feedback is a gift that can lead to growth and improvement.

Together, they explore the different types of feedback loops, from formal performance reviews to informal check-ins and peer evaluations. They discuss the importance of creating a safe space for feedback, where employees feel empowered to share their thoughts and ideas without fear of judgment or reprisal.

As they delve deeper into the discussion, Alex feels a sense of

clarity building within him. By integrating feedback loops for continuous improvement, they are not only identifying areas for growth and development but also fostering a culture of accountability and transparency that will drive organizational success.

As they brainstorm ideas and develop strategies to embed feedback loops into their day-to-day operations, Alex feels a renewed sense of purpose and determination. With Sarah by his side and the support of their colleagues, he knows that they are well-equipped to lead the HR department towards a future defined by learning, innovation, and sustainable success. Together, they will continue to innovate, adapt, and pave the way for a future filled with endless possibilities, drawing inspiration from the transformative power of feedback-driven continuous improvement.

Encouraging Experimentation and Risk-taking

In the dynamic meeting room, Alex and Sarah lead their team through an invigorating exploration of encouraging experimentation and risk-taking. Surrounded by screens displaying innovation labs and creative workshops, they embark on a journey to cultivate a culture where bold ideas are nurtured, and calculated risks are embraced.

As they initiate the discussion, Alex feels a surge of excitement. This is their chance to inspire their team to push beyond their comfort zones, to challenge the status quo, and to embrace failure as a natural part of the innovation process.

But encouraging experimentation and risk-taking is not just about encouraging wild ideas—it's about creating an environment where calculated risks are celebrated, and failures

CHAPTER 13: CONTINUOUS IMPROVEMENT

are seen as opportunities for learning and growth.

Yet Sarah remains steadfast, her belief in the power of experimentation and her willingness to embrace failure guiding the team through the complexities of fostering creativity. With her leadership, Alex learns to approach the challenge with courage and resilience, recognizing that true innovation requires a willingness to take risks and learn from setbacks.

Together, they explore the different ways to encourage experimentation and risk-taking, from providing resources and support for innovative projects to celebrating and rewarding bold ideas and initiatives. They discuss the importance of creating a safe space for failure, where employees feel empowered to take risks without fear of judgment or reprisal.

As they delve deeper into the discussion, Alex feels a sense of liberation building within him. By encouraging experimentation and risk-taking, they are not only unlocking the full potential of their team but also fostering a culture of creativity, resilience, and innovation that will drive organizational success.

As they brainstorm ideas and develop strategies to embed experimentation and risk-taking into their organizational DNA, Alex feels a renewed sense of purpose and determination. With Sarah by his side and the support of their colleagues, he knows that they are well-equipped to lead the HR department towards a future defined by boldness, creativity, and sustainable success. Together, they will continue to innovate, adapt, and pave the way for a future filled with endless possibilities, drawing inspiration from the transformative power of experimentation and risk-taking.

Creating Space for Creativity and Ideation

In the vibrant meeting room, Alex and Sarah guide their team through an inspiring exploration of creating space for creativity and ideation. Surrounded by screens displaying brainstorming sessions and design thinking workshops, they embark on a journey to cultivate an environment where imagination flourishes, and innovative ideas take root.

As they initiate the discussion, Alex feels a wave of excitement. This is their chance to unleash the creative potential of their team, to break free from the constraints of routine, and to foster a culture where every voice is heard, and every idea is valued.

But creating space for creativity and ideation is not just about scheduling brainstorming sessions—it's about fostering an atmosphere where curiosity is encouraged, and diversity of thought is celebrated.

Yet Sarah remains steadfast, her belief in the power of creativity and her commitment to fostering a culture of innovation guiding the team through the complexities of implementation. With her leadership, Alex learns to approach the challenge with openness and enthusiasm, recognizing that the most groundbreaking ideas often emerge from unexpected places.

Together, they explore different strategies for creating space for creativity and ideation, from establishing dedicated brainstorming sessions to providing opportunities for cross-disciplinary collaboration and knowledge sharing. They discuss the importance of creating a supportive environment where employees feel empowered to share their ideas and experiment with new approaches.

As they delve deeper into the discussion, Alex feels a sense of liberation building within him. By creating space for creativity and ideation, they are not only unlocking the creative potential of their team but also fostering a culture of innovation, collaboration, and inclusivity that will drive organizational success.

As they brainstorm ideas and develop strategies to embed creativity and ideation into their organizational culture, Alex feels a renewed sense of purpose and determination. With Sarah by his side and the support of their colleagues, he knows that they are well-equipped to lead the HR department towards a future defined by imagination, innovation, and sustainable success. Together, they will continue to innovate, adapt, and pave the way for a future filled with endless possibilities, drawing inspiration from the transformative power of creativity and ideation.

Implementing Processes for Evaluating and Scaling Innovation

In the forward-thinking meeting room, Alex and Sarah lead their team through an insightful exploration of implementing processes for evaluating and scaling innovation. Surrounded by screens displaying project management tools and innovation frameworks, they embark on a journey to establish a systematic approach to assessing and expanding groundbreaking ideas.

As they initiate the discussion, Alex feels a surge of anticipation. This is their chance to transform innovative concepts into tangible outcomes, to ensure that promising ideas are nurtured and scaled to drive meaningful impact across the organization.

But implementing processes for evaluating and scaling innovation is not just about implementing rigid protocols—

it's about striking the right balance between structure and flexibility, allowing for experimentation and adaptation while ensuring accountability and alignment with organizational goals.

Yet Sarah remains steadfast, her strategic vision and her commitment to excellence guiding the team through the complexities of implementation. With her leadership, Alex learns to approach the challenge with pragmatism and foresight, recognizing that the success of innovation initiatives hinges on effective planning, execution, and evaluation.

Together, they explore different methodologies for evaluating and scaling innovation, from setting clear criteria for success to establishing metrics for tracking progress and impact. They discuss the importance of fostering a culture of continuous learning and adaptation, where feedback is used to refine and improve innovative initiatives over time.

As they delve deeper into the discussion, Alex feels a sense of purpose building within him. By implementing processes for evaluating and scaling innovation, they are not only maximizing the potential of their innovative ideas but also building a foundation for sustained growth and success.

As they brainstorm ideas and develop strategies to embed these processes into their organizational culture, Alex feels a renewed sense of determination. With Sarah by his side and the support of their colleagues, he knows that they are well-equipped to lead the HR department towards a future defined by innovation, resilience, and sustainable success. Together, they will continue to innovate, adapt, and pave the way for a future filled with endless possibilities, drawing inspiration from the transformative power of evaluating and scaling innovation.

CHAPTER 13: CONTINUOUS IMPROVEMENT

Sustaining Momentum Through Ongoing Innovation Efforts

In the bustling meeting room, Alex and Sarah steer their team through an invigorating discussion on sustaining momentum through ongoing innovation efforts. Surrounded by screens displaying project timelines and innovation roadmaps, they embark on a journey to keep the momentum alive and propel their organization forward through continuous innovation.

As they kickstart the conversation, Alex feels a surge of energy. This is their chance to instill a sense of urgency and excitement, to ensure that their innovative initiatives don't lose steam but instead gather momentum with each stride forward.

But sustaining momentum through ongoing innovation efforts is not just about launching new projects—it's about fostering a culture where innovation is ingrained into the DNA of the organization, where every team member is empowered to contribute ideas and drive change.

Yet Sarah remains steadfast, her unwavering dedication to progress and her belief in the power of collective innovation guiding the team through the intricacies of sustaining momentum. With her leadership, Alex learns to approach the challenge with resilience and determination, recognizing that true innovation requires a long-term commitment and a willingness to embrace change.

Together, they explore different strategies for sustaining momentum through ongoing innovation efforts, from establishing innovation champions to fostering cross-functional collaboration and knowledge sharing. They discuss the importance of celebrating small wins and milestones along the way, keeping morale high and motivation strong.

As they delve deeper into the discussion, Alex feels a sense of purpose building within him. By sustaining momentum through ongoing innovation efforts, they are not only staying ahead of the curve but also driving continuous improvement and growth across the organization.

As they brainstorm ideas and develop strategies to embed innovation into the fabric of their organizational culture, Alex feels a renewed sense of optimism. With Sarah by his side and the support of their colleagues, he knows that they are well-equipped to lead the HR department towards a future defined by innovation, resilience, and sustainable success. Together, they will continue to innovate, adapt, and pave the way for a future filled with endless possibilities, drawing inspiration from the transformative power of ongoing innovation efforts.

14

Chapter 14: Building Resilience Through Efficiency

Understanding the Connection Between Efficiency and Resilience

The team convenes in a unique setting for today's meeting: a serene botanical garden on the outskirts of the city. The peaceful environment, filled with lush greenery and the gentle sound of water from a nearby fountain, is the perfect backdrop for a discussion on resilience.

Alex starts the conversation, his voice thoughtful as he gazes at the blooming flowers around them. "In nature, we see the perfect example of resilience. Plants adapt to their environment, finding ways to thrive even in harsh conditions. There's a lot we can learn from this."

Sarah, sitting cross-legged on the grass, nods. "Efficiency and resilience are deeply interconnected. Efficient systems allow us to respond swiftly and effectively to disruptions, just like these plants respond to changes in their environment."

Grace, the HR specialist, adds, "Resilience isn't just about bouncing back from challenges; it's about being prepared and adaptable. When our systems are efficient, they provide a strong foundation that helps us withstand and recover from setbacks."

Marcus, always enthusiastic about technology, chimes in. "Think about our IT infrastructure. When it's optimized and running smoothly, it can handle spikes in demand or unexpected failures. Efficiency ensures that we have the capacity and flexibility to maintain operations under stress."

Priya, the quality control expert, looks around the garden thoughtfully. "In our quality control processes, efficiency means reducing waste and ensuring consistent quality. This consistency builds trust with our customers and suppliers, which is crucial when facing disruptions."

Daniel, the senior analyst, speaks up. "Data is another key aspect. Efficient data management allows us to quickly analyze and respond to changing conditions. It helps us make informed decisions, even in the face of uncertainty."

The conversation flows naturally, inspired by the tranquil surroundings. They discuss how efficient resource allocation ensures that critical functions are always supported, even during crises. They explore how streamlined communication channels enable swift coordination and decision-making when it matters most.

As the sun begins to set, casting a warm glow over the garden, Alex brings the discussion to a close. "Efficiency isn't just about doing things faster or cheaper. It's about creating systems that are robust and adaptable. It's about being prepared for the unexpected and having the capacity to not only survive but thrive."

Sarah stands, a notebook in hand, and smiles at the team. "Let's document our thoughts from today and incorporate them into our overall strategy. By understanding the connection between efficiency and resilience, we can build an organization that's not only efficient but also capable of weathering any storm."

They spend the next hour capturing their insights and ideas, jotting them down in Sarah's notebook. They outline strategies for enhancing efficiency in ways that also bolster resilience, from improving supply chain flexibility to investing in robust IT systems and fostering a culture of adaptability.

As they leave the garden, the team feels a renewed sense of purpose. They've gained a deeper understanding of how their efforts in building efficient systems contribute to the resilience of their organization. They're not just preparing for the future; they're fortifying their foundation to ensure they can thrive, no matter what challenges come their way.

The next few weeks see these ideas put into action. The team works on optimizing various processes, from production to communication, with resilience in mind. They conduct training sessions to ensure everyone understands the importance of efficiency in building a resilient organization. They also set up regular review meetings to assess their progress and make necessary adjustments.

In time, their organization becomes a model of efficiency and resilience. They navigate challenges with confidence, supported by systems that are both streamlined and adaptable. The botanical garden visit remains a turning point, a reminder of the natural resilience they aspire to emulate. Their journey continues, guided by the principles of efficiency and the strength it brings.

Identifying Vulnerabilities in Systems and Processes

In the focused meeting room, Alex and Sarah lead their team through a meticulous examination of identifying vulnerabilities in systems and processes. Surrounded by screens displaying workflow diagrams and risk assessment matrices, they delve into the crucial task of identifying potential weaknesses that could compromise organizational resilience.

As they delve into the discussion, Alex feels a sense of urgency permeating the room. This is their opportunity to uncover hidden vulnerabilities lurking within their systems and processes, to proactively address weaknesses before they escalate into significant risks.

But identifying vulnerabilities in systems and processes is not just about pinpointing flaws—it's about cultivating a culture of transparency and accountability, where every team member plays a role in identifying and mitigating risks.

Yet Sarah remains steadfast, her strategic mindset and her meticulous attention to detail guiding the team through the complexities of vulnerability assessment. With her leadership, Alex learns to approach the challenge with precision and vigilance, recognizing that the ability to anticipate and address vulnerabilities is essential for building organizational resilience.

Together, they explore different methodologies for identifying vulnerabilities, from conducting thorough risk assessments to analyzing historical data and soliciting input from frontline employees. They discuss the importance of fostering a culture where team members feel empowered to speak up about potential issues and collaborate on solutions.

As they delve deeper into the discussion, Alex feels a sense of

determination building within him. By identifying vulnerabilities in systems and processes, they are not only strengthening the organization's ability to withstand challenges but also laying the groundwork for continuous improvement and growth.

As they brainstorm ideas and develop strategies to integrate vulnerability assessment into their organizational practices, Alex feels a renewed sense of purpose. With Sarah by his side and the support of their colleagues, he knows that they are well-equipped to lead the HR department towards a future defined by resilience, adaptability, and sustainable success. Together, they will continue to innovate, adapt, and pave the way for a future filled with endless possibilities, drawing inspiration from the transformative power of identifying vulnerabilities in systems and processes.

Developing Contingency Plans for Potential Disruptions

In the focused meeting room, Alex and Sarah guide their team through an intense discussion on developing contingency plans for potential disruptions. Surrounded by screens displaying risk scenarios and response strategies, they delve into the critical task of preparing for unforeseen events that could threaten organizational resilience.

As they delve into the discussion, Alex feels a sense of gravity settling over the room. This is their opportunity to anticipate potential disruptions, to formulate proactive strategies, and to ensure the organization's ability to respond swiftly and effectively in times of crisis.

But developing contingency plans for potential disruptions is not just about preparing for worst-case scenarios—it's about instilling confidence and clarity, empowering the team to navigate uncertainty with resilience and resolve.

Yet Sarah remains steadfast, her strategic acumen and her unwavering focus guiding the team through the complexities of contingency planning. With her leadership, Alex learns to approach the challenge with foresight and determination, recognizing that the ability to adapt and pivot in the face of adversity is essential for organizational survival.

Together, they explore different approaches to developing contingency plans, from scenario planning and tabletop exercises to establishing communication protocols and allocating resources for emergency response. They discuss the importance of agility and flexibility, allowing the organization to quickly mobilize and execute response plans as needed.

As they delve deeper into the discussion, Alex feels a sense of empowerment building within him. By developing contingency plans for potential disruptions, they are not only mitigating risks but also building a foundation for resilience and sustainability.

As they brainstorm ideas and develop strategies to integrate contingency planning into their organizational culture, Alex feels a renewed sense of purpose. With Sarah by his side and the support of their colleagues, he knows that they are well-equipped to lead the HR department towards a future defined by adaptability, agility, and sustainable success. Together, they will continue to innovate, adapt, and pave the way for a future filled with endless possibilities, drawing inspiration from the transformative power of developing contingency plans for potential disruptions.

CHAPTER 14: BUILDING RESILIENCE THROUGH EFFICIENCY

Strengthening Supply Chains and Infrastructure

In the strategic meeting room, Alex and Sarah lead their team through a comprehensive discussion on strengthening supply chains and infrastructure. Surrounded by screens displaying supply chain maps and infrastructure assessments, they delve into the critical task of fortifying the organization's logistical backbone to enhance resilience.

As they dive into the discussion, Alex feels a sense of determination pulsating through the room. This is their opportunity to bolster the organization's supply chains and infrastructure, ensuring they can withstand disruptions and continue operations seamlessly.

But strengthening supply chains and infrastructure is not just about shoring up physical assets—it's about forging resilient partnerships, optimizing processes, and leveraging technology to create a robust network that can adapt to changing conditions.

Yet Sarah remains steadfast, her strategic vision and her keen understanding of supply chain dynamics guiding the team through the complexities of enhancement. With her leadership, Alex learns to approach the challenge with foresight and innovation, recognizing that the strength of their supply chains is crucial for maintaining operational continuity.

Together, they explore different strategies for strengthening supply chains and infrastructure, from diversifying supplier networks to investing in digitalization and automation. They discuss the importance of building redundancies and alternative routes, allowing the organization to navigate disruptions with agility and efficiency.

As they delve deeper into the discussion, Alex feels a sense of

empowerment building within him. By strengthening supply chains and infrastructure, they are not only safeguarding the organization's operations but also positioning it for long-term growth and success.

As they brainstorm ideas and develop strategies to integrate supply chain resilience into their organizational practices, Alex feels a renewed sense of purpose. With Sarah by his side and the support of their colleagues, he knows that they are well-equipped to lead the HR department towards a future defined by adaptability, resilience, and sustainable success. Together, they will continue to innovate, adapt, and pave the way for a future filled with endless possibilities, drawing inspiration from the transformative power of strengthening supply chains and infrastructure.

Leveraging Technology for Resilience-Building Efforts

In the innovative meeting room, Alex and Sarah steer their team through an engaging discussion on leveraging technology for resilience-building efforts. Surrounded by screens displaying digital solutions and technological innovations, they delve into the pivotal role of technology in fortifying the organization's ability to withstand disruptions.

As they delve into the discussion, Alex feels a sense of anticipation filling the room. This is their opportunity to harness the power of technology to enhance resilience, to embrace digital solutions that can streamline operations, facilitate remote work, and enable rapid adaptation to changing circumstances.

But leveraging technology for resilience-building efforts is not just about implementing new tools—it's about fostering a culture of innovation and digital transformation, where technology is seen as a strategic enabler for organizational resilience.

Yet Sarah remains steadfast, her strategic foresight and her expertise in digitalization guiding the team through the complexities of technology integration. With her leadership, Alex learns to approach the challenge with creativity and ambition, recognizing that technology has the potential to revolutionize the way they operate and respond to disruptions.

Together, they explore different technological solutions for resilience-building, from cloud-based systems and remote collaboration tools to predictive analytics and artificial intelligence. They discuss the importance of investing in digital infrastructure and cybersecurity measures, ensuring that their technology ecosystem is robust and secure.

As they delve deeper into the discussion, Alex feels a sense of excitement building within him. By leveraging technology for resilience-building efforts, they are not only modernizing their operations but also future-proofing the organization against emerging threats and challenges.

As they brainstorm ideas and develop strategies to integrate technology into their resilience-building initiatives, Alex feels a renewed sense of purpose. With Sarah by his side and the support of their colleagues, he knows that they are well-equipped to lead the HR department towards a future defined by innovation, adaptability, and sustainable success. Together, they will continue to innovate, adapt, and pave the way for a future filled with endless possibilities, drawing inspiration from the transformative power of leveraging technology for resilience-building efforts.

Cultivating Adaptability and Agility in the Face of Challenges

In the dynamic meeting room, Alex and Sarah lead their team through a spirited discussion on cultivating adaptability and agility in the face of challenges. Surrounded by screens displaying agile methodologies and change management frameworks, they delve into the essential task of fostering a culture that embraces change and responds swiftly to adversity.

As they dive into the discussion, Alex feels a sense of energy pulsating through the room. This is their opportunity to instill a mindset of adaptability and agility, to empower their team to navigate uncertainty with resilience and creativity.

But cultivating adaptability and agility is not just about reacting to challenges—it's about proactively seeking opportunities for growth, learning, and innovation in the face of adversity.

Yet Sarah remains steadfast, her unwavering commitment to progress and her belief in the power of resilience guiding the team through the complexities of adaptation. With her leadership, Alex learns to approach the challenge with openness and determination, recognizing that adaptability and agility are essential for organizational survival in a rapidly changing world.

Together, they explore different strategies for cultivating adaptability and agility, from fostering a growth mindset and encouraging experimentation to providing training and support for skill development. They discuss the importance of creating a supportive environment where team members feel empowered to take risks and learn from failure.

As they delve deeper into the discussion, Alex feels a sense of optimism building within him. By cultivating adaptability and agility, they are not only preparing the organization to weather storms but also positioning it to thrive in the face of uncertainty.

As they brainstorm ideas and develop strategies to embed adaptability and agility into their organizational culture, Alex feels a renewed sense of purpose. With Sarah by his side and the support of their colleagues, he knows that they are well-equipped to lead the HR department towards a future defined by resilience, innovation, and sustainable success. Together, they will continue to innovate, adapt, and pave the way for a future filled with endless possibilities, drawing inspiration from the transformative power of adaptability and agility.

15

Chapter 15: The Future of Efficiency: Towards Sustainable Success

Reflecting on the Journey Towards Efficiency

In the contemplative meeting room, Alex and Sarah lead their team through a reflective discussion on the journey towards efficiency. Surrounded by screens displaying milestones and achievements, they take a moment to pause and look back on how far they've come, the challenges they've overcome, and the lessons they've learned along the way.

As they begin the discussion, Alex feels a sense of nostalgia washing over him. This is their opportunity to acknowledge the hard work and dedication that has brought them to this point, to celebrate their successes and reflect on the experiences that have shaped them.

But reflecting on the journey towards efficiency is not just about reminiscing—it's about distilling wisdom from past experiences, recognizing patterns, and identifying opportunities for growth and improvement.

Yet Sarah remains steadfast, her thoughtful perspective and her ability to see the bigger picture guiding the team through the process of reflection. With her leadership, Alex learns to approach the task with humility and gratitude, recognizing that every challenge they've faced has been an opportunity for growth.

Together, they revisit key moments in their journey towards efficiency, from the early days of experimentation to the strategic pivots and breakthroughs that have propelled them forward. They reflect on the obstacles they've encountered and the innovative solutions they've developed to overcome them.

As they delve deeper into the discussion, Alex feels a sense of pride swelling within him. By reflecting on their journey towards efficiency, they are not only honoring the hard work and dedication of their team but also gaining valuable insights that will guide them towards even greater success in the future.

As they share stories and lessons learned, Alex feels a renewed sense of camaraderie and purpose. With Sarah by his side and the support of their colleagues, he knows that they are well-equipped to continue pushing the boundaries of efficiency and sustainability, paving the way for a future filled with endless possibilities. Together, they will continue to innovate, adapt, and inspire others to join them on the journey towards a more efficient and sustainable world.

Celebrating Achievements and Milestones

In the jubilant meeting room, Alex and Sarah lead their team through a joyous celebration of achievements and milestones. Surrounded by screens displaying accolades and success stories, they take a moment to bask in the glow of their collective accomplishments, acknowledging the hard work, dedication, and perseverance that have brought them to this point.

As they begin the celebration, Alex feels a sense of pride swelling within him. This is their opportunity to honor the achievements and milestones they've reached on their journey towards efficiency, to recognize the contributions of every team member who has played a part in their success.

But celebrating achievements and milestones is not just about patting themselves on the back—it's about fostering a sense of camaraderie, unity, and pride within the team, fueling their motivation and commitment to continue pushing the boundaries of excellence.

Yet Sarah remains steadfast, her infectious enthusiasm and her ability to rally the team guiding the celebration with grace and charm. With her leadership, Alex learns to approach the task with humility and gratitude, recognizing that every achievement is a testament to the collective effort and collaboration of their team.

Together, they reminisce about the highlights of their journey towards efficiency, from major project milestones to individual triumphs and breakthroughs. They laugh, they cheer, and they share stories of challenges overcome and victories earned.

As they bask in the warmth of their shared success, Alex feels a deep sense of gratitude and appreciation for his team. By celebrating their achievements and milestones, they are not only honoring their hard work and dedication but also reinforcing their commitment to excellence and innovation.

As they raise a toast to the future, Alex feels a renewed sense of energy and determination. With Sarah by his side and the support of their colleagues, he knows that they are well-equipped to continue pushing the boundaries of efficiency and sustainability, paving the way for a future filled with endless possibilities. Together, they will continue to innovate, adapt, and inspire others to join them on the journey towards a more efficient and sustainable world.

Reinforcing the Importance of Sustainability and Long-Term Success

In the earnest meeting room, Alex and Sarah lead their team through a heartfelt discussion on the importance of sustainability and long-term success. Surrounded by screens displaying environmental impact reports and future projections, they emphasize the critical role of sustainability in shaping the organization's legacy and ensuring its continued prosperity.

As they delve into the discussion, Alex feels a sense of gravity settling over the room. This is their opportunity to reinforce the organization's commitment to sustainability, to emphasize that their journey towards efficiency is not just about short-term gains but about creating a lasting impact for future generations.

But reinforcing the importance of sustainability and long-term success is not just about rhetoric—it's about embedding these values into the organization's culture, operations, and decision-making processes, ensuring that they remain central to everything they do.

Yet Sarah remains steadfast, her unwavering dedication to sustainability and her visionary outlook guiding the discussion with passion and conviction. With her leadership, Alex learns to approach the task with sincerity and determination, recognizing that their actions today will shape the world of tomorrow.

Together, they reflect on the environmental and social implications of their work, from reducing carbon emissions to promoting social equity and inclusivity. They discuss the importance of setting ambitious sustainability goals and holding themselves accountable for achieving them.

As they delve deeper into the discussion, Alex feels a sense of purpose stirring within him. By reinforcing the importance of sustainability and long-term success, they are not only aligning their organization with global sustainability goals but also ensuring that they leave behind a legacy they can be proud of.

As they brainstorm ideas and develop strategies to integrate sustainability into their organizational practices, Alex feels a renewed sense of optimism. With Sarah by his side and the support of their colleagues, he knows that they are well-equipped to lead the HR department towards a future defined by sustainability, resilience, and prosperity. Together, they will continue to innovate, adapt, and pave the way for a future filled with endless possibilities, drawing inspiration from the transformative power of sustainability and long-term success.

Empowering Readers to Continue Their Efficiency Journey

In the inspiring meeting room, Alex and Sarah conclude their discussion by empowering their team to continue their efficiency journey. Surrounded by screens displaying motivational quotes and action plans, they instill a sense of confidence and determination in each team member, encouraging them to carry the torch of efficiency forward.

CHAPTER 15: THE FUTURE OF EFFICIENCY: TOWARDS SUSTAINABLE...

As they wrap up the discussion, Alex feels a surge of pride in his team. This is their moment to inspire and motivate others to embark on their own efficiency journey, to share their experiences and insights, and to empower others to make a positive impact in their organizations and communities.

But empowering readers to continue their efficiency journey is not just about offering advice—it's about igniting a spark of inspiration, providing practical tools and strategies, and nurturing a supportive community where individuals can learn, grow, and thrive together.

Yet Sarah remains steadfast, her unwavering belief in the power of collective action and her genuine desire to see others succeed guiding the conversation with warmth and empathy. With her leadership, Alex learns to approach the task with humility and compassion, recognizing that their journey is not just about themselves but about uplifting others and creating positive change in the world.

Together, they share their personal insights and lessons learned from their efficiency journey, from the challenges they've faced to the triumphs they've celebrated. They offer practical tips and strategies for overcoming obstacles and staying motivated, emphasizing the importance of perseverance, resilience, and collaboration.

As they conclude the discussion, Alex feels a sense of fulfillment wash over him. By empowering readers to continue their efficiency journey, they are not only paying it forward but also building a legacy of positive impact and transformation.

As they bid farewell to their team, Alex feels a deep sense of gratitude and appreciation. With Sarah by his side and the support of their colleagues, he knows that they have the power to inspire others to join them on the journey towards a more efficient and sustainable future. Together, they will continue to innovate, adapt, and pave the way for a future filled with endless possibilities, drawing inspiration from the transformative power of empowerment and collective action.

Offering Final Words of Advice and Encouragement

In the serene meeting room, Alex and Sarah offer their team final words of advice and encouragement as they conclude their discussion. Surrounded by screens displaying images of teamwork and success, they take a moment to impart wisdom and motivation to their colleagues, leaving them with a sense of purpose and determination as they continue their journey towards efficiency.

As they begin their closing remarks, Alex feels a sense of gratitude for the opportunity to lead and inspire others. This is their chance to offer guidance and support to their team, to reassure them that they have the skills, knowledge, and resilience to overcome any challenge that comes their way.

But offering final words of advice and encouragement is not just about giving instructions—it's about fostering a sense of camaraderie, empathy, and mutual respect, ensuring that each team member feels valued and empowered to make a difference.

Yet Sarah remains steadfast, her compassionate demeanor and her genuine care for others shining through as she shares her own insights and experiences. With her leadership, Alex learns to approach the task with authenticity and empathy, recognizing that their words have the power to uplift and inspire others.

Together, they offer words of wisdom and encouragement,

drawing from their own experiences and the lessons they've learned along the way. They remind their team to stay true to their values, to never lose sight of their goals, and to always be open to learning and growth.

As they conclude their final words, Alex feels a sense of pride in what they've accomplished together. By offering advice and encouragement to their team, they are not only guiding them towards success but also building a community of support and solidarity.

As they bid farewell to their colleagues, Alex feels a deep sense of gratitude and optimism. With Sarah by his side and the support of their team, he knows that they have the power to overcome any challenge and achieve their dreams. Together, they will continue to inspire, lead, and pave the way for a future filled with endless possibilities, drawing inspiration from the transformative power of teamwork and shared purpose.

Looking Ahead to the Ongoing Pursuit of Sustainable Success through Efficiency

As the meeting draws to a close, Alex and Sarah turn their gaze towards the future, looking ahead to the ongoing pursuit of sustainable success through efficiency. Surrounded by screens displaying images of innovation and progress, they inspire their team to remain steadfast in their commitment to driving positive change and making a lasting impact in the world.

With a sense of anticipation, Alex begins to speak, his voice filled with determination and hope. This is their moment to envision the future, to imagine the possibilities that lie ahead, and to chart a course towards a more sustainable and prosperous tomorrow.

But looking ahead to the ongoing pursuit of sustainable success through efficiency is not just about setting goals—it's about fostering a mindset of continuous improvement, innovation, and resilience, ensuring that they remain agile and adaptable in the face of uncertainty.

Sarah, ever the visionary, chimes in, her eyes alight with passion and purpose. With her guidance, Alex learns to embrace the journey ahead with optimism and courage, recognizing that their efforts today will lay the foundation for a brighter future for generations to come.

Together, they paint a picture of the future they aspire to create—a future where organizations operate in harmony with the planet, where prosperity is shared equitably, and where innovation drives positive change. They speak of the challenges that lie ahead, but also of the opportunities that await those who are bold enough to seize them.

As they conclude their discussion, Alex feels a sense of excitement building within him. By looking ahead to the ongoing pursuit of sustainable success through efficiency, they are not only envisioning a better future but also committing themselves to making it a reality.

As they bid farewell to their team, Alex feels a deep sense of purpose and determination. With Sarah by his side and the support of their colleagues, he knows that they have the power to shape the future they desire. Together, they will continue to innovate, collaborate, and lead the way towards a more sustainable and prosperous world, drawing inspiration from the transformative power of efficiency and sustainability.

About the Author

Goodson Mumba is a multifaceted individual known for his diverse expertise and prolific contributions across various fields. As an infopreneur, thought leader, and spiritual leader, he has inspired countless individuals through his insightful teachings and impactful writings. Mumba is also an accomplished author, with several notable works to his name, including "Understanding Corporate Worship," "The Years I Spent in a Week," "Management By Harmony," "The CEO's Diary," "Change to Change" and "Creative Thinking for results" His literary works span topics ranging from business management to personal development and spirituality, reflecting his broad range of interests and insights.

With a Master of Business Leadership (MBL) and a Bachelor of Arts in Theology (BTh), Mumba brings a unique blend of business acumen and spiritual wisdom to his work. His educational background is further enriched by a Group Diploma in Management Studies, providing him with a solid foundation in organizational dynamics and leadership principles. Additionally, Mumba holds diplomas in Education Psychology,

Leadership and Management Styles, Organizational Behaviour, Financial Accounting, Economic Growth and Development, and Project Management, showcasing his commitment to continuous learning and professional development.

Mumba's expertise extends beyond traditional academic disciplines, encompassing areas such as Neuro-Linguistic Programming (NLP) and Positive Psychology. His diverse skill set is complemented by a range of certifications, including Creative Problem Solving and Decision Making, Life Coaching Fundamentals and Techniques, Professional Life Coaching, and Performance Management System Design. These certifications reflect Mumba's dedication to equipping himself with the tools and knowledge necessary to empower others and drive positive change.

As an author, Mumba's writings reflect his deep understanding of human nature, organizational dynamics, and spiritual principles. His works offer practical insights, actionable strategies, and inspirational guidance for individuals seeking personal growth, professional success, and spiritual fulfillment. Mumba's holistic approach to life and leadership resonates with readers worldwide, making him a respected figure in both the business and spiritual communities.

Overall, Goodson Mumba's diverse background, extensive knowledge, and profound insights make him a sought-after speaker, mentor, and author. His commitment to excellence, lifelong learning, and service to others continues to inspire individuals to unlock their full potential and lead lives of purpose and significance.

Goodson Mumba is renowned for initiating the concept of Management by Harmony, revolutionizing traditional management practices with a focus on balanced and holistic approaches. He has authored two influential books on this subject: "Introduction to Management by Harmony" and its sequel, "Management by Harmony."

Mumba's work has significantly impacted the field, offering innovative strategies for fostering organizational harmony and efficiency. His contributions continue to shape contemporary management theories and practices.

www.ingramcontent.com/pod-product-compliance
Lightning Source LLC
Chambersburg PA
CBHW071830210526
45479CB00001B/65